Crossing the Line

Crossing the Line

Interracial Couples in the South

Robert P. McNamara, Maria Tempenis,
and Beth Walton

PRAEGER

Westport, Connecticut
London

The Library of Congress has cataloged the hardcover edition as follows:

McNamara, Robert P.
   Crossing the line : interracial couples in the South / Robert P.
McNamara, Maria Tempenis, and Beth Walton.
      p.   cm.—(Contributions in sociology, ISSN 0084–9278 ; no.
125)
   Includes bibliographical references and index.
   ISBN 0–313–30962–0 (alk. paper)
   1. Interracial marriage—South Carolina. 2. Interracial marriage—
South Carolina—Public opinion. 3. Public opinion—South Carolina.
4. Interpersonal relations—South Carolina. 5. South Carolina—Race
relations. I. Tempenis, Maria, 1974– . II. Walton, Beth, 1975–
. III. Title. IV. Series.
HQ1031.M395   1999
306.84′6′09757—dc21   98–44221

British Library Cataloguing in Publication Data is available.

A hardcover edition of *Crossing the Line* is available from
Greenwood Press, an imprint of Greenwood Publishing Group, Inc.
(Contributions in Sociology, Number 125; ISBN 0–313–30962–0).

Library of Congress Catalog Card Number: 98–44221
ISBN: 0–275–96676–3

First published in 1999

Praeger Publishers, 88 Post Road West, Westport, CT 06881
An imprint of Greenwood Publishing Group, Inc.

Printed in the United States of America

The paper used in this book complies with the
Permanent Paper Standard issued by the National
Information Standards Organization (Z39.48–1984).

10 9 8 7 6 5 4 3 2 1

To our parents
who tried to teach us
that most things in life are not simply
Black or White

Contents

Contents

Illustrations

Preface

In many ways, interracial couples represent one of the most fundamental features of American society: diversity. At the same time, however, they serve as symbols of one of the most unappealing American characteristics: racism. To be fair, our attitudes about interracial couples are changing in that we have become less concerned about people from different races marrying each other. However, this cannot be said of all regions of the country. The South, particularly South Carolina, with its long legacy of slavery and memories of an era when life was rather different from its present form, generally holds strong sentiments against changes in traditional family patterns.

The present study attempts to understand how one type of interracial relationship, Black/White married couples, living in the upstate region of South Carolina, cope with these negative attitudes. This is true both from the public and from members of the couples' respective families. What we have discovered tells us a number of deeply seated fears remain about people who marry someone from a different race, and this fear translates into a significant amount of social isolation for the couples.

In the minds of many people, these couples have crossed the line—they have violated generations of traditions and the implications threaten the very foundation of social life in their communities.

While the actual impact is far short of these dramatic depictions, the practical difficulties of participating in an interracial relationship are clearly documented in this study. Our goal is to offer a sociological account of what is taking place as well as trying to understand how and in what ways Black/White couples manage their lives.

Acknowledgments

Like most research projects, ethnographic or qualitative research is the type of venture in which the success of the project is heavily dependent on the cooperation of others. This is especially true of one's respondents, since the researcher asks them to give so much of themselves in order to understand their way of life. This project is no exception. Without the cooperation of the couples, who were willing to put aside their fears and concerns and spend considerable amounts of time with us, plus the inconvenience of subsequent visits and telephone calls to clarify and probe a bit deeper, this project simply would not be possible. To them we extend our sincerest thanks. We would also like to thank Jerry Massengill from the Probate Court for his help in locating interracial couples from marriage licenses in Greenville and the staff at Mount Zion Church, who put us in contact with several couples.

A host of others played an important role in this project. For instance, Freda Beatty of Furman University was of immeasurable help by providing us with insight into this population and offering her assistance in a variety of ways. With her help, our understanding of interracial couples was considerably enhanced. Additionally, a few colleagues merit our thanks, particularly Lloyd Benson, Steve O'Neill and A.V. Huff of Furman University. They are first rate scholars, wonderful friends, and as historians, helped us to understand how the history of the South, and South Carolina in particular, has shaped people's attitudes about interracial couples. We would also like to thank Steve Richardson and Wendy Moore of the Furman University library for their assistance and invaluable help. Similarly, we would like to thank the staff at the South Carolina Office of Public Health Statistics and Information Systems, particularly Mina Scott Barnes.

Finally, we would like to thank all those students who participated in the project as part of the Race and Ethnic Relations course. Their enthusiasm and insight prompted us to continue the study and learn more about this population. These students: Melissa Caron, Melinda Smith, Anthony Smith, Nicole Brokaw Wood, Gina Carreno, Sonya Henley, Jennifer Park, Allison Peck, Orlando Ruff, Bronwen Sanderson, and Kim Tongberg, deserve a great deal of credit for this project as well as our thanks. More recently, we owe a debt of thanks to Elizabeth Joseph and Andrea Mills for their insight and assistance. For those we have neglected or overlooked, please know you have our gratitude.

Chapter 1

The Nature of Black/White Relationships

Interracial couples. The very term evokes powerful emotions in some people. In others, it causes confusion or concern. In essence, the issues surrounding interracial couples are a reflection of the ways in which race operates in American society. The problems and difficulties many interracial couples experience only underscore the legacy of slavery and mistreatment of all minority groups.

On the surface, race seems to be such a simple concept. It can be defined as those physical characteristics that distinguish one group of people from another. It is also simple in the sense that there are, arguably, only three categories of racial groups (Caucasian, Black, Asian). However, there are a host of problems with the meaning of race. Many sociologists point to the ways in which these physical characteristics come to be defined—what is referred to as *the social construction of race*. Others take issue with the purity of the concept: it is virtually impossible to distinguish where one race ends and the next begins. As a result of these and other issues, some scholars have argued that we abandon the term altogether (see for instance Siegel 1998).

Thus, the concept of race is actually quite complex and the issues surrounding it become much more focused (and problematic) when individuals from different races become involved in intimate relationships (dating and/or marriage). For our purposes, we define an interracial couple as consisting of an African American and a White partner. The reason is that it not only avoids confusion regarding what we mean by interracial, but it also avoids the seemingly endless debate over whether or not race is the appropriate term to use. As was mentioned, this issue has been controversial in many disciplines, and rather than adding fuel to the debate, we chose to define our group in a way that most people could easily understand. Additionally, given the ways African Americans historically have been treated in the South, this type of union, and the problems that are generated from it, were of particular interest to us.

ATTITUDES ABOUT INTERRACIAL COUPLES

It would seem that the United States, with its history and heterogeneous population, would be tolerant of intimate relationships between people of different races. However, while it is true the number of interracial marriages has been increasing in this country, there is considerable debate over whether or not they are considered acceptable. In their study of college campuses, Stimson and Stimson (1979) found that 33% of White females and 33% of Black females were willing to date members of another race. They also found that 67% of Black males and 43% of White males were willing to date members of another race. The authors concluded that as negative attitudes towards interracial marriage declined, there would be a greater willingness to tolerate not only interracial dating, but marriage as well. This, in turn, would improve race relations across all groups. More recently, Rosenblatt, Karis, and Powell (1995) contend that the significant increase in the number of interracial marriages and dating indicates a greater tolerance toward relationships between people of different races. This can also be interpreted to mean racism in America is declining.

On the other hand, some researchers have suggested that the number of couples, although increasing, has remained small in part because of a lack of societal acceptance (see for instance Johnson and Warren 1994; Staples 1992). In other words, many experts have argued that Americans are strongly opposed to interracial relationships, particularly between African Americans and Whites. The reasons for this vary, but part of the explanation is found in stereotypical images of African Americans as well as the reasons why they intermarry with Whites.

MISCONCEPTIONS ABOUT INTERRACIAL COUPLES

A great deal of misinformation exists concerning interracial couples, especially why individuals would want to become involved in this type of relationship. While these explanations can be applied to virtually any minority group, they are most clearly seen with Black/White couples. Perhaps the most often cited reason is that African Americans date and marry Whites to escape their current financial and social situation: when an African American marries a White, it is a step toward upward social mobility.

Mills (1996) argues that while largely inaccurate, this statement contains an element of truth. From an economic standpoint, if an African American female marries a White male, there exists the possibility of upward social and economic mobility because White men earn, on average, more than African American men. However, since the vast majority of Black/White relationships involve African American men and White women, and since White women earn substantially less, on average, than men in general, this type of relationship does not benefit the African American. This pattern, particularly among African American males and White females led to a theoretical explanation of interracial marriages. Often referred to as a "hypogamy" theory, it is postulated by both Robert K. Merton and Kingsley Davis and given some support by Robert Staples. This explanation essentially states that African American males are attracted to White females because this type of relationship improves the social standing of the male. The same is true of White women who are attracted to higher status African American males. In short, the parties are "marrying up" (Billingsley 1992). The problem with Davis's and Merton's theory is that it is based on a pair of assumptions. First, it assumes the choice of marriage partner is based on quantifiable factors such as income and education. Second, it is also based on the assumption that most, if not all, Black men want to marry White women, but do not possess the means to do so. The real problem with the theory, as Spickard (1989) notes, is that it simply does not provide an adequate explanation of interracial marriage.

Another popular conception concerning interracial couples involves those individuals who rebel against their families by becoming involved with someone from a different race. This may have some basis if a person's family is racist and would clearly oppose this type of relationship. However, in those instances where the families support the couple, the rebellion argument loses much of its validity.

A related explanation suggests that people involved in multiracial relationships are either traitors of their own race or, at the very least, are diluting their racial identity. Parenthetically, Mills (1996) contends that this suggests many African Americans involved in interracial relationships dislike themselves. A similar argument is used to explain the behavior of Whites. It is often implied that a White who marries a Black is considered mentally ill for doing so (Frankenburg 1993). Thus, the White partner is considered unstable and the Black has demonstrated a lack of loyalty to African American culture.

A fourth perception about interracial couples implies that the basis of the relationship is sexual. The reason for the union has more to do with a preoccupation with what Staples and Johnson (1993) define as "forbidden fruit." This applies especially to White women and Black men. Here the historical connotations linger: during slavery, Blacks were forbidden to have intimate relationships with White women. Somehow, Mills (1996) sarcastically notes, this preoccupation of centuries ago has manifested itself in Black males' desire for White women in contemporary society. The same historical logic is used to explain the attraction of White men to Black women. That is, during slavery, it was a relatively common practice for White males to become sexually involved with Black females. This sexual allure of Black women continues today when White males act on their fascination and develop relationships with African American women.

Finally, and somewhat related to many of these explanations, some believe many interracial couples, particularly public figures, flaunt their relationship for the shock value or to engage in exhibitionism. However, studies have shown that, in general, many multiracial couples tend to avoid drawing attention to themselves and are often unwilling to participate in research on the subject for fear of being labeled and stigmatized (Kerwin et al. 1993; Rosenblatt, Karis, and Powell 1995).

In general then, there is an element of truth to some of the previously stated reasons why people from different races marry. However, it is one thing to suggest that individuals marry for economic and social benefits, to rebel against their parents, because of some internal mechanism of self-loathing, or simply for the shock value; it is quite another to suggest these motivations are the exclusive domain of interracial couples. Every reason cited, and others not mentioned, can be used to describe the motivations for all types of marriages.

For example, women who marry affluent men of the same race are considered to have *married well*—it is considered socially acceptable. Others who marry for convenience or because they are iconoclastic are praised as self-directed individualists who "march to the beat of a different drummer." Yet the same logic, when applied to people of different racial backgrounds, they are considered promiscuous, immoral, or irrational.

Tucker and Mitchell-Kernan (1990) challenge many of these conventional perceptions, particularly the upward mobility argument. In their study, they did not find significant differences in the characteristics of African Americans who married Whites compared to single race marriages. Intermarriage seems most likely to occur among middle class partners, among more African American men than women, more in the Western states than the South, and finally, with a greater age difference between partners.

OTHER FACTS ABOUT INTERRACIAL RELATIONSHIPS

While the subject of race is one of the most frequently discussed in the sociological literature, and while there is ample research concerning intermarriage among Europeans and other ethnic and religious groups (see for example Healey 1995; Kivisto 1995; Feagin and Feagin 1993; Marger 1994), surprisingly little attention has been given to intermarriage between African Americans and Caucasians (see for instance Rosenblatt, Karis, and Powell 1995; Mathabane and Mathabane 1992; Stuart and Abt 1975). Part of the reason for this may be the small number of cases as well as how the data is collected on interracial couples. While the information collected on interracial couples is not comprehensive or, in some cases, systematic (Porterfield 1982), the U.S. Bureau of Census provides perhaps the best tool with which to quantitatively measure this population. According to the Census Bureau, there were 65,000 Black/White married couples in 1970 and 326,000 in 1995.

As Table 1.1 indicates, interracial marriages increased from 65,000 in 1970 to 167,000 by 1980, which was roughly a 125% increase. By 1990, the number rose to 211,000 followed by another jump in 1995 to 326,000. While the number of Black/White marriages makes up one half of one percent of the estimated 55 million marriages in this country, a careful reading of this data shows that the number of Black/White married couples tripled from 1970 to 1990 and quintupled from 1970 to 1995. Thus, although still small in total numbers, Black/White marriages are increas-

Table 1.1
Ten Year Trends in Interracial Couples: 1970–1995 (in thousands)

TYPE	1970	1980	1990	1995
All Races	310	651	964	1,392
Black/White	65	167	211	326
Black hus./ White wife	41	122	150	204
White hus./ Black wife	24	45	61	122
White/ other race	233	450	720	988
Black/ other race	12	34	33	76

Source: *Statistical Abstract of the United States, 1996*; U.S. Department of
        Commerce, Bureau of the Census, *Current Population Reports*, pp.20–
        450.

ingly becoming a common feature of the social landscape (Staples and
Johnson 1993; Nakao 1993). Additionally, the proportion of Black men
married to White women has increased even more, quintupling from 1960
to 1990. And the trend is even clearer if one examines new marriages. In
1993, about 9% of Black men who married that year married a White
woman.

For African American women who marry White men, the rate was
slightly less than half of African American men, but it too is increasing
dramatically (Besharov and Sullivan 1996). Thus, the most common
Black/White marriage involves a Black male and a White female. Table

Table 1.2

Changes in Interracial Marriages: 1970–1995 (in thousands)

TYPE	1970	1984	1986	1988	1990	1995
Black hus./ White wife	41	111	136	149	150	204
White hus./ Black wife	24	45	64	45	61	122

Source: U.S. Department of Commerce, Bureau of the Census, *Current Popula-tion Reports, Population Characteristics, Household and Family Charac-teristics, March 1984, 1986, 1988, 1990.*

1.2 elaborates on Table 1.1 by showing incremental changes in the number of Black husbands and White wives. It shows an increase from 41,000 in 1970 to 111,000 in 1984. The number increased to 136,000 in 1986 to 149,000 in 1988 and to 150,000 in 1990 (Billingsley 1992). Among Black wives with White husbands, the numbers are distinctly smaller: from 24,000 in 1970 to 45,000 in 1980, 64,000 in 1986 and 45,000 in 1988. In 1990, the number rose to 61,000 and jumped again to 122,000 in 1995.

In South Carolina, the most comprehensive data on Black/White marriages is derived by the National Center for Health Statistics's *Vital Statistics of the United States.* According to this report, the number of interracial couples in South Carolina in 1996 was 869. This consisted of 618 African American males marrying White females and 251 White men marrying African American women. Like the national figures, the number of interracial couples has increased in the state and the data clearly shows that the African American male/White female type of interracial marriage is the most common. As Table 1.3 shows, the number of Black/White couples has increased three and a half times between 1977 and 1996. And while there has been a decrease in the number of Black/White marriages between 1994 and 1996, the decline is small, only about nine percent. Like the national figures, the number of White males who marry African American females nearly quintupled between 1977 and 1996 in South Carolina, while the number of Black males marrying White females has increased only about threefold in

Table 1.3
Changes in Black/White Marriages in South Carolina: 1977–1996

TYPE	1977	1983	1989	1994	1996
Black/White	247	421	751	953	869
Black hus./ White wife	194	293	524	687	618
White hus./ Black wife	53	128	227	266	251

Source: South Carolina Department of Health and Environment Control, Office of Public Health Statistics and Information System, a Division of Biostatistics.

that same period. This is in contrast to the national figures which show about a fivefold increase in both types of marriages.

In an attempt to answer the question of why the rate for African American women is only half that of African American men, Besharov and Sullivan (1996) offer a couple of possible explanations. First, women are more likely to select a spouse on the basis of earning capacity or ambition, while men are more likely to choose on the basis of physical attraction.

Another reason for the lower number of Black women marrying White men has to do with children. A woman with children is much less appealing to a male, irrespective of her race. Additionally, the data clearly shows that African American females are more than twice as likely as Whites to have had a baby out of wedlock.

Still another trend in interracial marriages is that, unlike in the past when they occurred later in life, often as second marriages, interracial couples today tend to marry earlier (Besharov and Sullivan 1996). Interestingly, for many White women, the interracial marriage is often their first. Besharov and Sullivan (1996) estimate the proportion of second marriages for Whites to a Black man was 33% in 1985, but only 22% by 1990, a decrease of one third.

Besharov and Sullivan (1996) also suggest that African Americans are substantially less likely to marry Whites than are Hispanics, Asians, or Native Americans. However, the increase in the number of couples could lead one to conclude that interpersonal racism is declining and African Americans are increasingly becoming attractive to other racial groups as potential mates. As African Americans continue to make strides in education and employment markets, their overall "marriage-ability," to other African Americans as well as to those from other races, improves.

Region of the Country

According to the 1990 Census, the five states with the most interracial couples are California, Florida, Oklahoma, Texas, and Washington. California, for example, had 26% of all interracial couples. As was mentioned, although the data on this issue is not comprehensive, interracial marriages are unevenly distributed to different parts of the country, with the West having the largest number. Tucker and Mitchell-Kernan (1990) offer an interesting explanation of this phenomenon.

Building off of social control theory, they contend the reason for the increase in interracial marriages is in part due to status enhancement. However, the real reason, especially for the higher incidence in the West than other parts of the county, has more to do with a weakened socialization from the various social institutions (family, schools, and peers) as people move away from their families of origin and their hometowns. In other words, the old social networks that operated to regulate a person's behavior no longer carry the same influence when they move away or change the groups with which they affiliate. As an illustration, in their study in Los Angeles they found that most of the people involved in interracial marriages were not born or raised in the city, they usually came from other parts of the country, most notably the Northeast, and from other parts of the world. In trying to explain not only the regional differences, but also why couples chose someone from another racial group, the authors state:

Systems of social control that discourage racial intermarriage, in particular, may exert greater influence on mate selection for first marriages than for subsequent marriages. The role of geographic mobility in this scheme is a function of one's social network. Moving usually means leaving behind relatives and friends, and establishing new relationships. (p.215)

Stability of Interracial Marriages

In terms of demographic variables, the research is fairly consistent: most interracial couples tend to be similar in social, educational, and occupational characteristics. Interracial couples also tend to be middle or upper class individuals. Additionally, in terms of housing, which is a factor in determining social class, the race of the husband determines where the couple lives. For instance, marriages involving White husbands typically resulted in the couple living in a White neighborhood and Black husbands typically bring their spouses to a Black neighborhood (see for instance Porterfield 1978; Billingsley 1992).

Related in some ways to socioeconomic status is the stability of the interracial marriage. Many who oppose these types of relationships believe them to be less stable than other, more conventional marriages. As Billingsley (1992) points out, the prevailing view in the literature is that this perspective has some validity, these marriages are less stable than marriages of two same race partners. Billingsley (1992) also contends that interracial marriages are at least three times less likely to succeed than single race families. Over twenty-five years ago, McDowell (1971) suggested the problem lies in the legacy of discrimination and racism in our society. The end result is that many interracial couples are simply incapable of withstanding the stress that accompanies the marriage. This point is echoed by others (see for instance Staples 1992; Billingsley 1992; Besharov and Sullivan 1996). As Staples (1992) states, "The 78% increase in divorce for whites during the past decade obviously indicates that they are encountering their share of problems with each other. Add to that the fact that intra-racial marriages have a considerably higher dissolution rate, it is clear that marrying across racial lines is no quick solution to the intractable problems of male-female conflict" (p.147).

On the other hand, some evidence suggests interracial marriages, depending on how they are defined, may be as stable as marriages with two Black partners, although they are less stable than marriages with two White partners (see for instance Monahan 1966; Mehta 1978). Unfortunately, the evidence on this subject is rather dated and the absence of recent research suggests that interest in this topic has waned.

While the relationship between marital stability and education is well known, meaning the higher the educational level of the partners, the higher the probability the marriage will survive for a long period of time, an interesting question is whether the same holds true for interracial couples. Billingsley (1992) finds that education is indeed a key factor in the stability of interracial marriages. Where husbands went beyond high school, the survival rate is so high among Black couples that it is virtually equal to the survival of White couples at the same educational level. Further, looking just at husbands with a college education, Black married couples (with husbands' education at the college level and beyond) had the highest survival rate, followed by Black husbands with White wives, while White husbands with Black wives had the lowest survival rate at this level of education. Thus, even educated interracial couples experience problems in sustaining their relationships.

Families

One of the most difficult aspects of participating in an interracial relationship is the reaction by each partner's family. Clearly, this can either place a tremendous strain on the couple or provide a haven of understanding and support for them. Tizard and Phoenix (1993) as well as Johnson and Warren (1994) found members of the immediate families of White partners were either hostile or fearful of the interracial relationship. Johnson and Warren (1994) also found members of a White partner's family typically tried to conceal the relationship from their friends, neighbors, and other family members where possible.

One explanation offered for this was the members may have been concerned about racism or perhaps they were concerned about the dilution of the all-White family. The authors speculate that, at some level, family members were concerned about losing their status or standing with other Whites who considered this type of relationship unacceptable. In sociological terms, this concealing was a form of face-saving and impression management (see Goffman 1969). The implications of this problem are far-reaching and can easily serve to isolate the White partner from their immediate and extended family. While feelings of rejection are understandable, especially if they are from one's immediate family, isolating oneself from the entire family precludes the possibility of any member accepting them. Thus, the underlying reason explaining White families' rejection of interracial relationships a fear of losing status and the concern about racism from associates and friends (Rosenblatt, Karis, and Powell 1995).

Fortunately, it appears that in those cases where there is opposition, there also seems to be a tendency for it to subside. While one or more family members would not initially accept the relationship, over time they became more tolerant and accepting of the African American partner (see for instance Kouri and Lasswell 1993; Tizard and Phoenix

1993; Rosenblatt, Karis, and Powell 1995). A good indicator of this acceptance was the willingness of the family member(s) to publicly acknowledge the relationship.

On the other hand, many Black families, for a variety of reasons, seem to be more accepting of interracial relationships. Part of the reason relates to the structure of the African American family, which can be very different from White families. As described by Rosenblatt, Karis, and Powell (1995) and supported by Staples (1992), mothers seem to be much more central to the family structure for African Americans. Additionally, since many African American families do not consist of both parents, they have a greater understanding of familial diversity. Consequently, African Americans encounter fewer problems with interracial relationships. This acceptance has been documented in other studies of interracial relationships as well (see for instance Kouri and Lasswell 1993; Porterfield 1978; Golden 1954). For instance, Golden (1954) found that, compared to White families, the families of African American partners in interracial relationships were much more able to see the White partner as a person rather than to react to him or her as a member of a group. Further, the relationship between the White partner and the African American's family tended to be much more lasting. While Golden's research is obviously dated, more recent research underscores many of his initial findings (see for instance Frankenberg 1993; Rosenblatt, Karis, and Powell 1995).

Thus, one way to interpret the reaction of families to the relationship is that initially, White families reject the African American partner, only to accept them to some degree as time passes (especially if the couple begins to raise a family), and African American families tend to be more accepting of interracial couples in general, but of those that reject them, feelings of hostility tend to linger for longer periods of time (Kouri and Lasswell 1993).

It may very well be that the deleterious effect of family opposition to interracial relationships is that the couple faces particular and somewhat unique stressors from each other. This could, in part, explain why interracial marriages are less stable than intra-racial ones. The couple already faces problems from society when they decide to enter into this type of relationship, adding the family opposition may result in a situation where the two individuals are unable to resolve their problems. While a certain amount of discord among in-laws is found in all types of families, it is particularly problematic for interracial ones given how race and racism are such fundamental parts of our society.

Children

One of the tempering mechanisms to family opposition, and, at the same time, a reason to oppose interracial relationships, has to do with children. But how many mixed racial children are there? This is obviously quite difficult to determine. For instance, many states no longer require that the parents' races be recorded on birth certificates. The Census Bureau estimates that in 1990, nearly 2 million children resided in homes where the primary adults were of different races (Besharov and Sullivan 1996). That is about 4.1% of the children who lived in two-parent households, about double the number since 1980, and four times the number in 1970. While this is only a rough estimate, we must also take into account those children who were adopted or are from a previous marriage. However it is calculated, there has been a significant increase in the number of interracial children in much the same way there has been an increase in the number of interracial marriages.

In general, the problems identified as relating to children of interracial relationships have to do with conflicts relating to social identity and self-identity. Stated differently, one of the major issues for interracial families is identifying, preserving, and explaining the cultural heritage to their children. Researchers have often conjectured that biracial children are at risk for developing a variety of problems (see for instance Adler 1987; Brandell 1988; Kerwin et al. 1993). Kerwin et al. (1993) in their study of Black/White biracial children, found that, in contrast to other research, children did not perceive themselves as marginal and demonstrated, as did the adults, strong feelings of sensitivity to the views, values, and culture of both Black and White communities.

Still, problems can and do emerge for biracial children. According to Ladner (1984), the issue of social identity among biracial children is dealt with in one of three ways. Parents may deny that race is an issue at all; they may promote minority identity in their children; or they may attempt to raise their children to understand the meaning and significance of a biracial identity.

Second, and perhaps more important, are the ways in which parents deal with the problems their biracial children face, both during childhood and later as young adults. All of these things can cause conflicts within the child in terms of his or her identity. McRoy and Freeman (1986) have found that many biracial individuals have a particularly difficult time during adolescence, due in part to the lack of a clearly defined social identity. Clearly, while much has been learned, there remain numerous questions about the critical issues associated with biracial children, particularly as it relates to their sense of self-identity.

THE PROBLEMS OF INTERRACIAL COUPLES

Despite what can be generally referred to as an increased acknowledgment of interracial couples, problems, some of which are quite serious, remain. One of the main purposes of this study is to explore the issues, both positive and negative, surrounding interracial couples as they understand them. While we will have more to say on the particular problems Southern couples experience, a few trends appear in the literature.

Perhaps one of the most common problems relates to members of the African American community itself. A great deal has been written about the concerns of African American women towards African American men and White women (see for instance Staples and Johnson 1993; Collins 1990). As was mentioned, while many African American males have not had successful attempts at the American Dream, which makes them less viable as marriage partners for African American women, there remains an image that African American males are being taken away from them.

Many African Americans feel that if a male member of their race marries a White, he is "selling out" his culture, his heritage, and his people. Still others view this as a rejection of Black women's beauty (Rosenblatt, Karis, and Powell 1995). Others feel African American males who marry White women are trying to gain economic and social standing through affiliation with the dominant group in society. In some cases, the attention is focused on White women who are "stealing" their men from them. Whether or not this is an accurate depiction, the realities of the situation mean that interracial couples involving a Black man and a White woman must somehow come to terms with the resentment from African American females.

Some members of the African American community feel that any interracial marriage is unacceptable, but especially ones involving Whites. The rationale behind this is the feeling that it is unacceptable to choose a partner that belongs to a group which historically and currently, exploits and denies opportunities to African Americans in general (Rosenblatt, Karis, and Powell 1995).

Other problems relate to discrimination and prejudicial behavior in public. This can consist of poor service at restaurants and motels, hostile stares, the loss of promotional opportunities in the workplace, or even dismissal for being involved in an interracial relationship. Further along the continuum are the outright physical and verbal attacks, receiving hate mail, death threats, or the burning of churches that welcome interracial couples. There is also anecdotal evidence of a fear of institutional racism operating: many couples are leery of revealing the nature of their relationship to government agencies. For example, Welborn (1994) discovered that many interracial couples refuse to list their race on marriage licenses.

Thus, the nature of the problems experienced by interracial couples are vast and range from simple stares to outright attacks against them. As was mentioned, we will have more to say on this in a separate chapter, but for now recognize that while it appears our sensitivity as a society toward interracial couples seems to be improving as evidenced by the increase in numbers of couples, there is a great deal left to understand.

METHODS

This ethnographic study consisted of in-depth interviews with 28 interracial couples in the upstate area of South Carolina. As one might imagine, locating couples who were willing to participate in the study was extremely problematic (see for instance Hammersley and Atkinson 1984; Agar 1980). There are no national data bases or membership lists one can use to find these individuals, although there are organizations in some states. As such, more creative means had to be employed, each with varying levels of success. Locating couples was only the first step in a rather complex process (see for instance Smith and Kornblum 1995). As was mentioned, many couples are reluctant to participate in studies for fear of retaliation or simply because they do not wish to be stigmatized with the "interracial" or "multiracial" label. In some cases, we discovered they had participated in other studies, only to have their confidences betrayed or had confidential information revealed.

Nevertheless, we began our efforts to identify couples with an analysis of marriage licenses. In the city of Greenville, South Carolina, these documents are a matter of public record and the information in the application included, among other things, the names of both parties, addresses, and race of each person. From these records, we were able to identify a list of approximately 150 Black/White couples who applied for a license during the 1996 year. From the addresses, we were then able to obtain the telephone numbers of the couples using the telephone book or directory assistance. However, upon attempting to contact these individuals, we encountered several problems.

In some cases the address was fictitious, while in others the address was valid, but the couple had simply used the address to complete the application, they had not lived there. In other cases, the couple had moved after they were married and did not leave a forwarding address. And finally, a number of couples had used the address of a relative, who, upon being contacted by us, would not reveal any information concerning the couple's residence. While the reasons for the misrepresentation of the addresses raise a number of interesting questions, especially as to why the couples fabricated information, we were still faced with the issue of finding couples willing to participate. From this original list obtained from the marriage licenses, we were able to secure only four interviews.

However, a former student, herself involved in an interracial relationship, told us about a local church that had several members who were involved in interracial relationships. From this group, almost all of whom participated, we were able to develop a snowball sample of their friends and/or relatives. We were also able to identify a support group for interracial couples sponsored by another local church. Unfortunately, the group did not hold meetings for several months during the year and eventually disbanded completely.

We also sent an e-mail message over the Internet explaining the project and how individuals who met the criteria could contact us. We then contacted two magazines in the Atlanta area with the hope of placing an ad in one of their issues. However, both magazines declined, stating they had recently amended their publishing policy to prohibit such ads. Finally, we placed an ad with a weekly alternative newspaper in Greenville. This resulted in two additional interviews.

In a number of cases, those who were willing to be interviewed were very gracious and candid in their responses: the couples typically invited us into their homes and some even made dinner for us. These interviews lasted, on average, approximately one and a half hours, with some as long as three hours. In addition to tape recording, handwritten notes were also taken; noting any observations, body language, interesting comments, or any information that could not be identified by recording. In the interest of safety, as well as comprehensiveness in data collection, most of the interviews were conducted by two of the three members of the research team. This technique also came in handy since one interviewer could concentrate on the interview while the other could make observations as well as develop a rapport with the children where applicable.

In a few situations, one member (McNamara) conducted interviews alone, but these were exceptional cases. Additionally, we varied our pairings to observe different interview styles and to ensure our intercoder reliability when analyzing the data. Later in the study, one author (McNamara) reinterviewed a number of couples, some by telephone, to gain additional insight and information. The data was transcribed and coded using *The Ethnograph*, a text-based software program which allows for content analysis.

As was mentioned, a number of methodological problems had to be addressed during the course of the study. For instance, in addition to being reluctant to participate in the project, a number of couples were hesitant to refer us to other couples unless they held similar views. We had to repeatedly stress that we were interested in all issues surrounding these types of relationships. We also reminded couples that sifting out the important pieces of information was our job and they could be doing a disservice to the study and our overall understanding by trying to limit our access only to those couples whose views coincided with their own.

Finally, a word or two on the use of terms is in order. In an effort to be sensitive to each couple, as well as members of each race, we use the terms African American and Black interchangeably. The reason for this has more to do with the way the couples themselves used it: they used both to mean African Americans, and as such, we felt it was appropriate to use it in the same way. The same is true with regard to the term interracial. Many of the couples we interviewed chose the term as the primary way to identify themselves. Others used multicultural to describe their relationship. In the course of subsequent chapters, we will also use these terms interchangeably.

While the following pages will describe the issues, both positive and negative, relating to interracial couples in the South, we should note that we do not attempt to generalize to the larger population. We have selected a small segment of the population that was not chosen randomly or with any degree of representativeness. Consequently, we make no claim to drawing a scientific sample and our observations and insights only apply to those we interviewed.

We should also note that the couples we interviewed represent only a certain segment of the interracial population. Since we relied on a snowball sampling technique and focused on married couples, and given the data on the instability of interracial marriages, it may be that those couples who experienced serious and significant problems ended up terminating their relationships. Consequently, by focusing on those individuals whose marriage remained intact, we may have captured a glimpse of one end of the continuum. These couples have endured the problems and found some way to overcome them and allow their relationships to grow. If we can identify problems and issues in these relationships, one can only speculate the deleterious effects they may have had on those couples who could not stay together.

In terms of the style of presentation, we have chosen, wherever possible, to let the couples recount their experiences, with all the richness and depth of detail. We do this because we feel it provides an important context of understanding. In short, we let them tell their stories, but also offer a running commentary through the discussion.

What must also be recognized is the problems experienced by interracial couples are a manifestation of the legacy of how these unions have been treated. In Chapter 2, we discuss the historical implications of interracial couples beginning with slavery and ending during the 1970s, a period of particular concern for individuals involved in these type of relationships. Interestingly, during this period most of what we currently know about interracial couples was discovered. In Chapter 3 we introduce some of the main characters of the study, including some background information to help us to understand who they are and how the couple met. In Chapter 4 we discuss the families of the couples and how they have reacted to the marriage and the introduction of biracial children. In Chapter 5 we focus on the problems our couples experienced, plus the various coping mechanisms they employ to minimize the impact these problems present. In Chapter 6 we explore some of the theoretical explanations of the phenomenon of interracial couples. Drawing from the seminal work of Gordon Allport (1947) and the research on the effects of the contact hypothesis, we attempt to place the problem in its proper sociological context. Additionally, we incorporate a discussion of the labeling theory of deviance as a way of identifying how and in what ways interracial couples consider themselves outcasts from mainstream society. Finally, in the Conclusion, we discuss the positive aspects of interracial relationships. As we will attempt to show, there are a variety of benefits, especially in terms of multiculturalism. Within this concluding chapter we also examine the future of interracial relationships and describe what interracial couples would like others to know about them.

REFERENCES

Adler, A. J. 1987. "Children and Biracial Identity," in A. Thomas and J. Grimes (eds.) *Children's Needs: Psychological Perspectives*. Washington, D.C.: National Association of School Psychologists.

Agar, M. 1980. *The Professional Stranger.* New York: Academic Press.

Allport, G. W. 1947. *The Nature of Prejudice*. Boston, MA: Beacon Press.

Besharov, D. J. and T. S. Sullivan. 1996. "America Is Experiencing an Unprecedented Increase in Black-White Intermarriage," *The New Democrat* July/August, pp. 19–21.

Billingsley, A. 1992. *Climbing Jacob's Ladder*. New York: Simon and Schuster.

Brandell, J. R. 1988. "Treatment of the Biracial Child: Theoretical and Clinical Issues," *Journal of Multicultural Counseling and Development* 16:176–187.

Collins, P. H. 1990. *Black Feminist Thought*. New York: Routledge.

Feagin, J. and C. Feagin. 1993. *Race and Ethnic Relations.* Clifton-Hills, NJ: Prentice-Hall.

Frankenberg, R. 1993. *White Women, Race Matters: The Social Construction of Whiteness.* Minneapolis, MN: University of Minnesota Press.

Goffman, E. 1969. *The Presentation of Self in Everyday Life*. New York: Anchor.

Golden, J. 1954. "Patterns of Negro-White Intermarriage," *American Sociological Review* 19: 144–147.

Hammersley, P. and D. Atkinson. 1984. *Principles of Ethnography*. London: Tavistock.

Healy, J. F. 1995. *Race, Ethnicity, Gender and Class.* Thousand Oaks, CA: Pine Forge.

Johnson, W. R. and D. M. Warren (eds.). 1994. *Inside the Mixed Marriage*. Lanham, MD: University Press of America.

Kerwin, C., J. Ponterotto, B. Jackson, and A. Harris. 1993. "Racial Identity in Biracial Children: A Qualitative Investigation," *Journal of Counseling Psychology* 40(2): 221–231.

Kivisto, Peter. 1995. *Americans All*. Belmont, CA: Wadsworth.

Kouri, K. M. and M. Lasswell. 1993. "Black-white Marriages: Social Change and Intergenerational Mobility," *Marriage and Family Review* 19(3/4):241–255.

Ladner, J. 1984. "Providing a Healthy Environment for Interracial Children," *Interracial Books for Children Bulletin* 15:7–8.

Marger, M. N. 1994. *Race and Ethnic Relations.* 3rd Edition. Belmont, CA: Wadsworth.

Mathabane, M. and G. Mathabane. 1992. *Love in Black and White*. New York: HarperPerennial.

McDowell, S. F. 1971. "Black-White Intermarriage in the United States." *International Journal of the Family* 1:57.

McRoy, R. G. and E. Freeman. 1986. "Racial Identity Issues Among Mixed-Race Children," *Social Work in Education* 8:164–174.

Mehta, S. K. 1978. "The Stability of Black-White vs. Racially Homogamous Marriages in the United States 1960–1970," *Journal of Social and Behavioral Science* 24:133.

Mills, C. 1996. "Interracial Marriage Is Identical to Same-Race Marriage," in Bonnie Szumski (ed.) *Interracial America: Opposing Viewpoints*, pp. 210–215. San Diego, CA: Greenhaven Press.

Monahan, T. 1966. "Interracial Marriage and Divorce in Kansas and the Question of Instability of Mixed Marriages," *Journal of Comparative Family Studies* Spring: 119.

Nakao, A. 1993. "Interracial Marriages on the Rise in State, US," *The San Francisco Examiner* February 12, p. A1.

Porterfield, E. 1978. *Black and White Mixed Marriages*. Chicago: Nelson-Hall.

——— . 1982. "Black-American Intermarriage in the United States," *Marriage and Family Review* 5(1):17–34.

Rosenblatt, P. C., T. A. Karis, and R. D. Powell. 1995. *Multiracial Couples*. Thousand Oaks, CA: Sage.

Siegel, B. 1998. "Anthropology and the Science of Race," in Robert P. McNamara (ed.) *Perspectives in Social Problems*. Boulder, CO: CourseWise Publishing.

Smith, C. and W. Kornblum (eds.). 1995. *In the Field*. 2nd edition. Westport, CT: Praeger.

Spickard, P.R. 1989. *Mixed Blood: Intermarriage and Ethnic Identity in Twentieth-Century America*. Madison, WI: University of Wisconsin Press.

Staples, R. 1992. "Black and White: Love and Marriage," in R. Staples, *The Black Family: Essays and Studies*. Belmont, CA: Wadsworth.

Staples, R. and L. B. Johnson. 1993. *Black Families at the Crossroads: Challenges and Prospects.* San Francisco: Jossey-Bass.

Stimson, A. and J. Stimson. 1979. "Interracial Dating: Willingness to Violate a Changing Norm," *Journal of Social and Behavorial Sciences* 25:36–44.

Stuart, I. R. and L. E. Abt. 1975. *Interracial Marriage: Expectations and Realities.* New York: Grossman Publishers.

Tizard, B. and A. Phoenix. 1993. *Black, White, or Mixed Race? Race and Racism in the Lives of Young People of Mixed Parentage*. New York: Routledge.

Tucker, B. and C. Mitchell-Kernan. 1990. "New Trends in Black American Interracial Marriage: The Social Structural Context," *Journal of Marriage and the Family* 52:209–218.

United States Department of Health and Human Services, National Center for Health Statistics. 1996. *Vital Statistics of the United States.* Washington, D.C.: U.S. Government Printing Office.

Welborn, M. 1994. "Black-white Couples: Social and Psychological Factors that Influence the Initiation, Development, and Continuance of their Relationship," Unpublished doctoral dissertation, University of Minnesota.

Chapter 2

Mulattoes, Miscegenation, and the History of Black/White Marriages

In the previous chapter we alluded to the increasing tolerance of Americans in the 1990s toward interracial marriages, as evidenced by the increasing number of interracial couples. However, the problems experienced by many of today's couples have a long and somewhat stormy past. Interestingly, mixed marriages are not as uncommon as most people think. As Williamson (1980) argues, the great majority of American Blacks are of mixed ancestry and the history of Blacks is also the history of Mulattoes. A *mulatto* was a person who was half black and half white. A *quadroon* was a person who was one-quarter black and an *octoroon* was someone who was one-eighth black. Miscegenation, which we will discuss at length, includes the mixing of Blacks and Mulattoes as well as the mixing of Whites with either Blacks or Mulattoes (Williamson 1980).

Over the sweep of history there has been strong opposition to interracial marriages. One explanation for this and the consequent anti-miscegenation laws, was to prevent the mongrelization of the races (Staples 1992). Others argued the laws were designed to protect the sexual purity of White women. While these laws were targeting Black men and White women, many historians argue this type of interracial sex was offensive not because of what it represented per se, but rather it was a threat to White power, particularly men (see for instance Spickard 1989; Williamson 1980; Roberts 1994). In contrast, while sexual relations between White men and Black women had been a relatively common occurrence, when Black men began taking White women as spouses it was perceived as a threat to the existing social structure (Staples 1992).

Having said this, it behooves us to recognize that these strongly held attitudes against interracial marriages were not absolute. Like the treatment of most minorities in this country, Americans have been willing to overlook some instances of both sexual relations and marriage, particularly when it involved White men of considerable station, and when it occurred on a relatively small scale. Thus, as was (and is) often the case, we were very willing to overlook some instances of what was perceived as an otherwise pernicious behavior when it was expedient or in our best interests.

At the same time, however, there is no discounting the level of intensity of these attitudes against interracial couples—their presence became threatening. This was particularly true in those instances when the number of interracial marriages increased.

A BRIEF HISTORY OF SLAVERY IN AMERICA

The African way of life itself was a stratified society which also entailed the institution of slavery. Slaves were usually people captured in war, were usually the property of the chief of the tribe or head of the family, and some were exported and sold to others. In America, Africans of different tribal cultures were uprooted and forced to live together leading to a unique African culture (Franklin 1980).

England quickly realized using only White servants in America was unacceptable. Shipping captured slaves from Africa became the solution though not more than one half of the slaves survived or became effective workers. This was due to a multitude of factors (e.g., disease, suicide, or jumping overboard) (Franklin 1980).

The first slaves in America, which consisted of twenty in Jamestown in 1619, were more like indentured servants. As more entered the new world, Whites began to fear the growing numbers of Blacks, which led to the creation of slave codes. By the mid-1700s, slavery was an integral part of the economic system in colonial America. By 1790, there were nearly 750,000 Negro slaves in America. With the South's development into a "cotton kingdom," slavery was integral to economic success and Southern thinking. The African slave trade flourished as did the systematic breeding of slaves. For instance, by 1796, many slave girls were mothers by the age of thirteen. Also during this time many farmers divided slave families because they were not economically profitable (Franklin 1980).

The slave population was concentrated into the hands of a relative few: of the 8 million Whites, only about 385,000 people owned slaves. Yet, slavery dominated in the South, primarily because most staple crops were produced on plantations by slave labor, which gave slave owners a significant amount of political power. The slaves themselves were treated as childlike and of an inferior race, and corporal punishment was often used to increase their labor productivity. Most slave children were allowed to play freely with White children until they reached a useful age and at such time playing was limited. By the time they reached a certain social age, interracial playing was terminated (Morgan 1975).

Negroes who were freed by their masters had to keep passes that verified their freedom. Still, various regulations limited their movement and the power of freedom still rested with the White man. For instance, if a White claimed the free Negro was really a slave, there was little recourse. There were also restrictions on what free Negroes could do to earn a living. For example, they could not sell corn, wheat, or tobacco without a license, which was almost impossible to obtain (Morgan 1975).

SLAVERY AND INTERRACIAL MARRIAGES

Staples (1992) contends that slavery had the greatest impact on interracial relationships since most of the slaves who came to this country were males. This imbalance of Black males to females led to an increased number of sex relations between Black males and indentured White women, some of which resulted in marriage. At one time, these types of marriages were considered profitable for Whites since any children created from this relationship were also slaves (Jordan 1968). However, note also that during the seventeenth century not all Blacks were slaves. Some were independent landowners and even employers of servants (Spickard 1989). Gradually, slavery became more of a common feature of the Black experience in this country. By the time large numbers of Africans were imported in the eighteenth century, in the minds of many Americans, being Black also meant being a slave (Spickard 1989).

It was during slavery that the frequency of interracial mating occurred on a wide scale. At this point in history, there were more men than women, particularly in the South. This, coupled with the unequal distribution of power in society, where the slaves and indentured servants were considered property, many relationships between White men and their Black female slaves went unpunished. While casual sex between Blacks and Whites posed little threat, marriage, on the other hand, suggested that the two parties were equal in status and social standing. This was intolerable and, for the most part, Whites were firmly opposed to interracial marriage (Spickard 1989). However, despite these attitudes and objections, most White men only received minor censure for engaging in sexual activity with Black females. It was in this type of system that White men also took Black concubines.

Concubines were slave women who entered into a more stable relationship with a White man, occasionally resulting in marriage, but usually the woman was returned to slave status after a period of time. The question remains as to whether or not concubines entered into these relationships willingly. While the woman would enjoy the prestige of being associated with the master and have better housing, food, clothing, love, and power over other slaves, some historical data suggests that duress may have been a factor. Since the data on this subject is mixed, it is fair to suggest at least some concubine relationships contained an element of coercion (Billingsley 1992; Spickard 1989).

Spickard (1989) notes that most of the sexual relations between White men and Black women in antebellum times involved slave women. But in certain southern cities, notably Charleston and New Orleans, free women of color took part in a fascinating pattern of social interaction. In New Orleans, for example, in a system known as *placage,* White men courted well-educated quadroon women, sometimes asked permission for marriage, agreed to purchase a home, and provided for any children created from the relationship. Much of this sympathetic understanding of interracial relationships was explained by the fact that New Orleans accepted different degrees of Whiteness and Blackness (i.e. mulatto, quadroon, octoroon, metis).

Places like New Orleans were clearly exceptions. Although the attitudes concerning mistresses and other types of relationships between White men and Black women was somewhat acceptable, far more difficult were legal marriages. Between 1798 and 1865, all the southern states and 14 Northern and Western states passed laws prohibiting marriages between Whites and Blacks or Whites and Mulattoes (Roberts 1994).

It was also during this period that people began to realize, unlike their counterparts in New Orleans and other cities, it was often difficult to distinguish some Blacks from Caucasians: the effects of intermingling of the races during previous generations was already being felt. Moreover, there had not been any consistency in defining who would be excluded from marriage to a White person. Some states defined it as one-fourth, others one-eighth and still others excluded anyone with any amount of African blood. This is often referred to as the *one drop rule* (Williamson 1980). The notion comes from a long discredited belief that each race has its own blood type, which was associated with physical appearances in addition to an individual's behavior. As Wright (1994) describes it, the antebellum South promoted the rule as a way of enlarging the slave population with the children of slave holders.[1]

Although Black/White relationships were socially stigmatized, evidence of the frequency with which Whites and Blacks were sexually involved with one another is found in the prevalence of Mulattoes, particularly in the South.

MULATTOES

Williamson (1980), in his analysis of the history of Mulattoes in the United States, argues much of what emerged as anti-miscegenation was really a reaction against the rising numbers of Mulattoes, who were then mixing with White women. The first significant mixing of Whites and Blacks came in the late seventeenth and early eighteenth centuries in the Chesapeake area of Virginia and Maryland. Most of the Mulattoes were said to be the children of White servants and Blacks.

The Whites were indentured servants of European descent, many of whom were repaying the costs of their travel to their new homeland in years of service rather than monetarily. In addition to those seeking a better life in America, a number of White criminals were sent to Chesapeake colonies. Given the menial nature of the work and the conditions under which they lived, these Whites had extensive contact with enslaved and free Blacks (Morgan 1975). For some, intimate relationships developed and the existence of Mulatto children was one of the results.

However, the colonies did not approve of interracial relationships and, especially for the first Mulattoes, could not come to a clear conclusion on what to do with them. In the mid 1600s, Virginia decreed that Mulatto children of slave mothers would themselves be slaves. Additionally, the state passed strict laws for anyone who engaged in a sexual relationship with a Black. However, Mulatto children of White women were a different problem. They were to be free, but community attitudes remained contentious. Virginia declared that the child of a White woman fathered by a Black or Mulatto would be sold as a servant until he or she reached the age of thirty (Williamson 1980). While not prohibiting interracial marriages, Virginia also ordered the White partner banished from the colony. Later, this penalty was increased to six months in jail. Still, this did not resolve the official standing of the person of mixed ancestry once he or she reached adulthood (after thirty years of age). In short, the overall treatment of Mulattoes in Virginia was severely restricted in terms of employment opportunities, owning property, or holding public office (Williamson 1980).

Other states soon followed the lead of their Virginia and Maryland neighbors. Pennsylvania went a step further in the early 1700s by prohibiting interracial marriages of any kind. In essence, the reaction to Mulattoes and anti-miscegenation laws probably had more to do with the idea of race mixing than the extent to which it was occurring. To underscore this point, Williamson (1980) argues that on the eve of the American Revolution, the number of Mulattoes in the Chesapeake region was approximately three percent of the total population.

In the antebellum years, the Mulatto population grew. While statistics are only available for the 1850 and 1860 Census, it is clear, even as a rough approximation, that this segment of the population was increasing. From 1850 to 1860, the number of Mulattoes increased from 405,751 to 588,363 (Spickard 1989). Additionally, a large percentage of Mulattoes were free because some White masters emancipated their slave children in addition to White women giving birth to free children by Black men.

There was also a distinct difference between the upper and lower regions of the South. The former consists of North Carolina and areas North and West of the state. In the upper South, Mulattoes appeared very early in the colonial period and in relatively large numbers. Moreover, as was mentioned, many Mulattoes in the upper South were free, although they tended to be poor or of only modest means. This group was treated as if they were Black. In the lower South, Mulattoes appeared later and some had affluent White fathers. As a result, many of them were provided with employment and even political opportunities. Some mulattoes were so light and privileged that the distinction between them and members of White society was almost imperceptible. For the most part, however, Mulattoes were treated as a third class by influential Whites, serving as a buffer between Whites and Blacks.

In 1850, most of the Mulattoes lived in the upper South, with upwards of 200,000, a third of which were free, while only about 90,000 lived in the lower South, of which only about ten percent were free. In the lower South, nearly all of the Mulattoes lived in New Orleans, Charleston, Mobile, and Savannah. In the upper South, the free Mulattoes remained in rural areas (Spickard 1989).

This concern with the Mulatto population peaked when many slaves, both Black and Mulatto, were being emancipated. States attempted to draw a clear line between them and Whites, particularly those in the privileged classes, and the new, but restricted privileges of free Blacks. In fact, in some cases, creditors and White family members protested wills which provided free status to slave children. In addition to the series of laws passed prohibiting interracial marriages, a body of laws also emerged that resulted in free Mulattoes being cast as second-class citizens (Woodson 1918). Woodson (1918) argues that the intent of anti-miscegenation laws was not so much to prevent sexual relations between Whites and Blacks, but "to debase to a still lower status the offspring of the blacks . . . to leave women of color without protection against white men" (p.350).

The South Carolina Experience

According to the 1850 Census, some 4,400 free Mulattoes lived in South Carolina, more than half of which lived in Charleston. A number of these families went on to become as affluent and cultured as their White neighbors. The basic reason for the large proportion of free Mulattoes in upper South the Black population increased as the number of indentured servants began to dissolve. At the same time, White women were increasingly taking Blacks or Mulattoes as mates.

However, this relaxed attitude towards interracial relationships was not unanimous. While some Whites publicly defended interracial marriage, interracial sex outside of marriage came under attack in both the press and the legislature. For instance, in 1717 an act of the assembly provided that "any white woman, whether free or a servant, that shall suffer herself to be got with child by a Negro or other slave or free Negro, . . . shall become a servant for . . . seven years." The children were to be bound for 21 years if male and 18 years if a female. White men who impregnated Negro women were also required to suffer the same penalty. In 1721, a law was passed that stated only free White men could vote, thus ending some voting by free Blacks and Mulattoes, reducing their impact on policy (Williamson 1980).

FACTORS IN EXPLAINING RATES OF MISCEGENATION

In an attempt to offer a historical explanation for interracial marriages, Williamson (1980) argues that four elements were needed. The first was simply getting White people and Black people together in the same geographic area. A large initial Mulatto population occurred when a number of Whites and Blacks were brought together. Where there were many Whites and few Blacks, such as in New England during this time, few Mulattoes were born. In colonial South Carolina, the area grew from a small colony, in which Whites outnumbered Blacks, to one in which Blacks comprised 51 percent of the population in 1708 and 70.6 percent just before the Revolution. With relatively few Whites present and the races only briefly evenly matched, it was fair to expect few Mulattoes in colonial South Carolina. During this period in Virginia, however, there were 306,000 Blacks, both slave and free, and approximately 452,000 Whites. Because the races were more closely matched, there were more Mulattoes here than in South Carolina.

Second, the rate of miscegenation was also influenced by sex ratios. For instance, by about 1700 the ratio of White men to White women was three to two. This imbalance existed at a time when large numbers of African slaves were flooding into the colony. There was also a sexual imbalance among Blacks in favor of men. This large number of Whites and Blacks, coupled with a sexual imbalance among Whites (in favor of White men) set in motion the process of creating a large Mulatto population (Williamson 1980).

Proximity was the third element used to explain high levels of miscegenation. This consists of people of one sex and race in close distance to people of the opposite sex and race. Finally, the rate of miscegenation was influenced by inclination. In the upper South, the ruling class had strong feelings against miscegenation, while the lower South accepted it and practiced it rather regularly.

There is an additional factor in understanding miscegenation that Williamson does not mention. This involves general perceptions of Blacks and Whites. As Spickard (1989) notes, these images have had a lasting impact in explaining the attitudes and behaviors the two groups have of each other.

Historically, many Whites held the view that Black men were simple and childlike, yet incredibly strong and virile, with an inclination towards violence. It has also been suggested that Black men are endowed with other traits: larger sex organs and an insatiable desire for sexual pleasure. Accompanying these characteristics is the belief that it is a lifelong goal of Black males to have sexual relations with White women. The juxtaposition of these traits, specifically the penchant for violence and a sexual preoccupation with White women, is clearly expressed in the reactions to the rape of White women by Black men. Throughout history, Black men have been accused of raping White women. Moreover, these fears and concerns were validated in media accounts and became, in some sense, part of American folklore.

While the perceptions of Black men elicit fear and intimidation, Black women have been perceived in two ways: as sex objects and as socially repulsive. Like Black males, in many cases, Black women have been historically viewed as insatiable in their sexual appetites. There are several accounts in which White men emphatically state that Black women are more passionate, more sexually alluring, and the source of many White men's fantasies (Spickard 1989). At the same time many White males laud the sexual prowess of Black females, there is also the understanding that most Black women are too "easy"—they were by their very nature, promiscuous. Of particular interest were Mulatto women. Inexplicably, to many White males, Mulatto women represented the ultimate in sexual fantasy.

Interestingly, the perceptions of White women by Blacks plays an important, if not overlooked role in understanding interracial relationships. In many ways, White women were (and are) the standards of beauty in our society by which all other women are compared. Whiteness is pure, clean, and virginal. Given that, it is indeed reasonable that *all* men, Black ones included, would pursue their passions with women with these characteristics (Spickard 1989).

For some Black men, White women are symbols of status, of beauty, something to be revered. At the same time, the images of White women by Black men may also contribute to this passion. Black men view White women as being nicer, more compassionate, and more enthusiastic about sex than Black women. They also believed White women would treat them as they think they should be treated. Obviously, these beliefs could easily result in finding White women more attractive (Spickard 1989).

Of all the groups' images, perhaps the Black perception of White men would be the easiest to understand. The most defining characteristic is the power White men possessed as a group throughout most of the century. The abuse of that power came in the form of rape, which caused many Black women to view White males with suspicion. This also led many Black women to reject the possibility of a relationship with a White man. However, not all Black women saw White men as predators or to be rejected as possible mates. Some Black women saw White men as more stable and dependable than Black men. Others regaled in being close to the power that White men wielded. Still, this represented a minority point of view and throughout history Black women were more resentful of the abuse committed by White men (Spickard 1989).

Spickard (1989) also argues that these images of Blacks and Whites were consistently applied throughout the post-slavery era and it has only been in the last 20 years or so that there has been a reconsideration of their validity.

THE POST-SLAVERY ERA

During Reconstruction, many anti-intermarriage laws were repealed or declared void. As Mangum (1940) describes, southern states that retained these laws were lax in their enforcement of them. Reuter (1931) has argued this resulted in increases in the number of marriages between Whites and Blacks. Despite the lack of legal restrictions however, there were serious social implications. The vast majority of White southerners vehemently opposed interracial marriages.

The period following Reconstruction in the South was characterized by a general increase in anti-Black hostility: the separate but equal distinctions in public institutions, and a reintroduction of anti-interracial marriage legislation (Roberts 1994). Those states which had not enforced their anti-miscegenation laws, or had them repealed during Reconstruction, reasserted their influence. While the original laws prior to the Civil War prohibiting interracial marriages classified someone as Black if they were one-fourth or one-eighth Black, many of these new laws became increasingly restrictive: some states prohibited the marriage if the person was one-sixteenth or, in some cases, any trace of Negro descent (Staples 1992). The penalties for violating this statute ranged from a fine of 100 dollars or more or up to ten years in prison (Mangum 1940; Wirth and Goldhamer 1944). Other penalties included whipping, enforced servitude, and banishment (Spickard 1989).

THE TURN OF THE CENTURY

By 1920, 30 states prohibited marriages between Whites and Blacks and this number remained constant until 1948 (Roberts 1994). In the South, there remained strong and hostile feelings about Black men marrying or dating White women. Many southerners believed that this type of relationship was a form of rape since no self-respecting White woman would willingly become involved with a Black man. As a result, Black men became extremely sensitive to any kind of public contact with White women for fear of severe retaliation by White men. Black men were beaten, hanged, dismembered, and dragged behind automobiles for having relationships with White women (Spickard 1989). In one sense, they were defeated no matter what behavior they exhibited. Should they be polite and friendly, it might have been perceived that they had ulterior motives and designs on the woman. And if they did not demonstrate the appropriate conduct toward White women, such as proper etiquette and deference, they could be retaliated against for being impolite.

It was also increasingly difficult for a White man to maintain a mistress in the South, therefore the Mulatto children which came from such unions often grew up in fatherless homes. One strategy employed by some interracial couples was to move north or to a state that had not passed anti-miscegenation laws (Roberts 1994). While there had been some improvement in the legal standing for many Blacks in the North, those strides did not extend to social status. To most northern Whites, Blacks remained a despised group, who were said to be inferior, and sorely limited in terms of economic opportunities. Thus, while there was no legal prohibition of interracial marriages in the North, it was still considered socially unacceptable.

As a result, between 1918 and 1939, there were few Black/White marriages, not because of a lack of interest, but because of this strong negative public sentiment against these types of relationships. However, some researchers have suggested that the impact of the public sentiment toward these types of relationships precluded the need for legislation (Spickard 1989). In lieu of formal mechanisms to prevent interracial marriages, informal social control operated, which led to the same result.

While the vast majority of research conducted on interracial couples during the early years, and continuing into the 1930s and 1940s, focused on the demographic characteristics, one particular study attempted to identify some of the problems interracial couples experienced during this period. In his study of Black/White couples in Chicago, Roberts (1940) found most people viewed Whites who married Blacks as members of the lowest class. They were often ostracized by relatives and friends, and were discriminated against in the same way Blacks had been with regard to employment and housing opportunities.

In terms of how the interracial couples met, Roberts (1940) found that the most common situation was through employment. The typical job involved domesticated labor, where one or both worked as servants in a home or as members of the housekeeping staff in hotels. These types of jobs required long hours and few opportunities to meet others. Roberts (1940) also found that despite the social stigmatization and other sanctions, and despite admitting to the costs associated with the relationship, a majority of interracial couples indicated they were happily married. In some ways, this could be taken as a rationalization, and, as we shall see, resolution of the social stigma associated with marrying someone from another race often comes in the form of a disregard for societal attitudes and values. Still, prior to World War II, this type of relationship was hidden from others for fear of a loss of status. This was particularly true with the White partner's family. If relatives did not outrightly reject their new Black in-laws, they kept this information from more distant family and friends.

Another important issue relating to interracial couples, then and now, was the prospect of being fired from a job should the employer learn the worker was involved in an interracial relationship. This was particularly true of White women (Roberts 1994). One way of coping with this threat was to withhold information about one's marital status. Couples often claimed they were single, lived in a different neighborhood, or provided a relative's telephone number to their employer in an effort to conceal their true identities.

The late 1930s was a time in which Blacks were socially and legally segregated within American society. It was the era of Jim Crow, which meant there were few opportunities for Whites and Blacks to meet and socialize, particularly those of the opposite sex (Roberts 1994). As was mentioned, 30 states had passed anti-interracial marriage laws and social hostility precluded such unions even where no law had been passed prohibiting it.

Over the next 30 years, particularly in the 1960s, American attitudes toward racial discrimination and segregation began to lessen, and an increase in the number of interracial marriages occurred (Billingsley 1992). Increasingly, Blacks came to be defined as an important part of American society and our social policies began to reflect that fact. In the 1940s and 1950s many cities and states created commissions and task forces targeting the problems associated with racial discrimination. As a result, by 1963, 21 states and more than 40 cities had passed fair employment practices laws (Staples 1992).

Similarly, Congress passed a series of Civil Rights Acts between 1957 and 1968 which guaranteed equal rights to Blacks and created programs such as affirmative action. As a policy, affirmative action was the positive effort to recruit minority group members or women for jobs, promotions, and educational opportunities. The phrase first appeared in an executive order issued by President Kennedy in 1963. The order called for contractors to take affirmative action to ensure that applicants are employed and that employees are treated during employment without regard to their race, creed, color, or national origin. Four years later, the order was amended to prohibit discrimination on the basis of sex, but affirmative action was still vaguely defined.

This plan, coupled with the Civil Rights movement, increased legislation abolishing the separate but equal doctrine of the past. Also, Supreme Court decisions which underscored the validity of these laws provided many Blacks with jobs and other opportunities on an unprecedented scale. The increased contact with different groups led not only to the development of diverse social networks, but also an increase in intermarriage. This is especially true in those states which had repealed their anti-miscegenation laws (see for instance Monahan 1970; Heer 1966; Lynn 1967).

In the South, the changing attitudes toward and treatment of Blacks was not well received. As Roberts (1940) describes, a " . . . second Reconstruction would be forced upon the South with civil rights legislation and judicial decisions removing all legally imposed racial segregation of public schools, means of transportation, restaurants, hotels, libraries, parks, theaters, and other places of public accommodation, and prohibiting restrictions on legal and political rights" (p.55). Most Whites perceived the new laws granting Blacks access to institutions and opportunities as threatening to their way of life. Of particular concern were voting rights and racial intermarriage (see for instance Mangum 1940). Already smarting from what they perceived as governmental meddling, Southerners did not need vivid examples of their changing way of life by having an interracial couple living in their midst (see for instance Lynn 1967). An unintended consequence of this new legislation and court decisions, both of which were designed to help Blacks, was a perilous situation for interracial couples living in the South.

By 1967, marriages between Whites and Blacks were increasing in the North and the West and only the 17 southern and border states still prohibited interracial marriages. In June of that year, the United States Supreme Court, in *Loving v. Commonwealth of Virginia*, 87 S. Ct. 1817 (1967) declared that the Virginia anti-intermarriage statute was unconstitutional in that it violated the Equal Protection Clause of the Fourteenth Amendment.

In June 1958, in Central Point, Virginia, a rural area where Blacks and Whites had mixed for generations, two residents, Mildred Jeter, a Black woman, and Richard Loving, a White man, were married in Washington, D.C., where interracial marriages were legal. Shortly thereafter, the Lovings moved back to Virginia. In October of that year, a grand jury issued an indictment against the Lovings, charging that they violated Virginia's laws prohibiting interracial marriages. The Lovings were convicted of violating Section 20–58 of the Virginia Code, which stated:

Leaving State to evade law.—If any white person and colored person shall go out of this State, for the purpose of being married, and with the intention of returning, and be married out of it, and afterwards return to and reside in it, cohabiting as a man and wife, they shall be punished as provided in Section 20–59, and the marriage shall be governed by the same law as if it had been solemnized in this State. The fact of their cohabitation here as man and wife shall be evidence of their marriage.

Section 20–59, defined the penalty for miscegenation. It stated:

Punishment for marriage.—If any white person intermarry with a colored person, or any colored person intermarry with a white person, he shall be guilty of a felony and shall be punished by confinement in the penitentiary for not less than one nor more than five years.

In January 1959, the Lovings pled guilty to the charge and were sentenced to one year in jail. However, the trial judge suspended the sentence for a period of 25 years on the condition that the Lovings leave Virginia and not return together for that same period of time.

After the conviction, the Lovings moved to Washington, D.C. In 1963 they petitioned the state trial court to set their sentences aside on the grounds that the statutes upon which they were convicted violated the Fourteenth Amendment to the U.S. Constitution. A year later, after no action had been taken, the Lovings filed a class action suit in the United States District Court to declare the law unconstitutional and to prevent state officials from enforcing their convictions. This motion was denied and the Lovings appealed to the Supreme Court of Appeals of Virginia. This court upheld the constitutionality of the anti-miscegenation statutes.

The basic reasons the appellate court did not reverse the lower court's decision were threefold. First, they felt the states had a legitimate purpose in "preserving the racial integrity of its citizens and to prevent a mongrel breed of citizens." Second, and related, the appeals court reasoned that marriage was traditionally regulated by the states and federal intervention was an unnecessary practice. Third, the appeals court felt, like the state court, that because its miscegenation statutes punished both the White and the Black participants in an interracial marriage, they did not violate the Equal Protection Clause.

In response, the U.S. Supreme Court overturned the appellate court's ruling. Chief Justice Warren, in writing the majority opinion, stated that miscegenation statutes designed to prevent marriages on the basis of racial classification violated both the Equal Protection and the Due Process Clauses of the Fourteenth Amendment. He states:

> There can be no question but that Virginia's miscegenation statutes rest solely upon distinctions drawn according to race. The statutes proscribe generally accepted conduct if engaged in by members of different races. Over the years, this Court has consistently repudiated "distinctions between citizens solely because of their ancestry" as being "odious to a free people whose institutions are founded upon the doctrine of equality." At the very least, the Equal Protection Clause demands that racial classification, especially suspect in criminal statutes, be subjected to the "most rigid scrutiny" and, if they are ever to be upheld, they must be shown to be necessary to the accomplishment of some permissible state objective, independent of the racial discrimination which it was the object of the Fourteenth Amendment to eliminate . . . There is patently no legitimate overriding purpose independent of invidious racial discrimination which justifies this classification. The fact that Virginia prohibits only interracial marriages involving white persons demonstrates that the racial classification must stand on

their own justification, as measures designed to maintain White Supremacy . . . There can be no doubt that restricting the freedom to marry solely because of racial classification violates the central meaning of the Equal Protection Clause.

Still, the Supreme Court decision in the *Loving* case did not cause the violent rift the *Brown* decision had nor did it open the floodgates for couples anxiously waiting for the repeal. Many southern states simply delayed voiding their statutes. In a few instances action had to be taken, such as in December 1970 when a federal judge ordered Alabama officials to stop enforcing their anti-interracial marriage statutes (Sickels 1972), but by and large, the level of resistance by the states was relatively low. It was almost as though the states had relented and accepted the legal inevitability.

Additionally, as Sickels (1972) discovered, there were only 32 interracial marriages in North Carolina and Virgina in 1967, and approximately the same number the following year. A few other studies in different states confirmed this trend, suggesting that the problems experienced by couples were not legal ones, although that was certainly part of it (see Monahan 1976). On the other hand, some evidence exists to suggest the impact of the *Loving* decision was rather significant. Annella (1967) collected information on marriage licenses in Washington, D.C. and found that, at a time when the total number of marriages was decreasing, the number of interracial ones increased dramatically. The number of interracial marriages jumped from 17 in the period of 1941–1945 to 177 from 1956–1960 to 493 from 1961–1965. Nationwide, the percentage of interracial marriages among Blacks doubled from 1960–1970. Additionally, the number of Black/White couples who married doubled between 1970 and 1980 from 77,000 to 168,000. Although small in absolute numbers, the percentages and the rates of interracial marriages have increased substantially. Thus, while some evidence appears to suggest that the *Loving* decision had little impact, other studies suggest a different trend.

While the issue of interracial marriage had been decided, the courts took longer to decide what to do about custody when an interracial couple divorced. It had been the historical practice in many states to terminate a divorced White woman's custody rights to her children if she remarried interracially. It took until 1984 for the Supreme Court, in overriding a Florida court, to rule out the use of race as a factor in custody cases (see "Blackburn v. Blackburn" 1982).

However, while small in number, and though it did not create great legal debates, the societal reaction in the South was significantly hostile. Williamson (1980), in describing the backlash, argues that Southerners were ill prepared for the psychological impact of these events. He contends that, for a long while, the efforts at reform really did not play an instrumental role in the lives of White America. Then, suddenly, the *Brown v. Board of Education* ruling is handed down, the Montgomery bus boycott takes place, followed by the demonstrations by Blacks during the 1960s. Then in 1967, the anti-miscegenation laws were struck down as well. To some, it was the final insult to the Southern way of life.

THE ROLE OF RESEARCH IN INTERRACIAL MARRIAGES

The 1920 Census was the last count of Mulattoes in the United States. After that, the Census no longer counted persons of mixed White and Black ancestry. It seems clear that where the Census began omitting data on mixed couples, the social science community responded by collecting data on them. This occurred at a time when sociologists and anthropologists became interested in race and the way it shaped and influenced social life. For instance, Edward Reuter (1918), a student of Robert Park at the University of Chicago, published one of the first books on Mulattoes.

W.E.B. Du Bois (1897) was a pioneer in the field and the first Black trained as a sociologist. In his fifteen month study during 1896 and 1897 of the condition of Blacks in Philadelphia, Du Bois surveyed 9,000 households and collected data on 33 interracial families. Of the 27 Black husbands, 19 were born in the South, and 15 of the White wives were born in foreign countries (six in Ireland, three in England and two in Scotland and Germany respectively). Du Bois concludes that:

It is often said that only the worst Negroes and the lowest Whites intermarry. This is certainly untrue in Philadelphia: to be sure among the lowest classes there is a large number of temporary unions and much cohabitation . . . On the other hand it is an error certainly in this ward to regard marriages of this sort as confined principally to the lower classes; on the contrary they take place most frequently in the laboring classes, and especially among servants where there is the most contact between the races. (p.358)

The social scientific understanding of race as a phenomenon was brought to light with Gunnar Myrdal's (1944) *An American Dilemma.* The basic question being asked here was who was mixing with whom? The conclusion was the Mulatto was not dying but rather mixing with parts of the Black population and evolving into what was referred to physically and culturally as the New Negro. Williamson (1980) refers to this as the *browning* of America. It was not so much that Blacks were mixing with Whites, but rather that Mulattoes were mixing with Blacks.

In examining the early sociological literature on interracial marriage, it seems apparent that much of the data is limited. Part of the problem was locating couples to study, and to do so with a representative sample. Unfortunately, then as now, the population does not lend itself to such analysis. However, of the studies conducted, most focused on demographic characteristics of the couples, such as the frequency of mixed marriages, and the sex and race of the marriage partners. Bruce and Rodman (1975) are quite critical of the research during this period. In fact, they contend it is impossible to draw conclusions from the research, particularly those studies that used convenience samples for their data. Additionally, the authors contend that even though these studies are conducted with nonrepresentative samples, they are institutionalized in the literature as being comprehensive in scope. They say:

Both Roberts' and Schulyer's studies are good examples of how nonrepresentative samples, over time, come to be referred to in the literature as being complete surveys of specific populations. Roberts' work does not include all Black-White marriages in Chicago between 1925–1938, but only the number of couples he was able to locate; nevertheless, many secondary sources incorrectly refer to his study as a complete survey. Perhaps the most dramatic example of grasping at straws and transforming them into data relates to the reports made of Schuyler's work. Many studies that present these data treat them as complete empirical surveys of Black-White marriages for Cleveland and twenty-two other cities. It turns out, however, that Schuyler's figures are based upon estimates made by Negro observers. There is no way of knowing anything about the accuracy of these estimates, and it seems far better to discount the figures than to transform them into population survey statistics. (p.155)

While we understand the frustration expressed by these authors, the nature of this topic limits access to researchers and limits the generalizability of the findings of many studies. This was particularly true in the early research on interracial couples, but the difficulties are apparent in contemporary studies as well. However, this does not invalidate the findings of any study—rather it means that building a substantial body of knowledge or theoretical understanding of interracial marriages is more difficult.

CONCLUSION

It appears then that the mixing of races between Blacks and Whites, whether it was in the context of marriage or some other form, has historical links tracing back to the very beginning of American society. The result has been an institutionalization of interracial relationships. The negative attitudes toward these types of relationships has remained strong and the problems created for Black/White couples have many far-reaching implications. Despite the fact that American society is more tolerant of interracial couples than perhaps at any other time in history, as evidenced by the increasing number of interracial marriages, the problems African Americans have experienced, directly and indirectly through the legacy of slavery, will forever cast them and their White spouses in a negative light. This is a group that remains stigmatized, whether or not they (or we) are willing to admit it. The focus of the subsequent chapters is to examine those issues and problems and to identify not only the way they are managed, but the future of these types of relationships as well.

NOTE

1. Parenthetically, this rule has contemporary implications. In 1986, the United States Supreme Court refused to review a lower court's decision that a Louisiana woman whose great-great-great-great grandmother had been the mistress of a French planter was Black—even though that proportion of her ancestry amounted to no more than 3/32 of her genetic heritage. As professor G. Reginald Daniel, who teaches at the University of California at Los Angeles states, "We are the only country in the world that applies the one-drop rule, and the only group that the one-drop rule applies to is people of African descent" (Wright 1994).

REFERENCES

Annella, M. 1967. "Interracial Marriages in Washington, D.C.," *Journal of Negro Education* 36:428–433.

Billingsley, A. 1992. *Climbing Jacob's Ladder*. New York: Simon and Schuster.

"Blackburn v. Blackburn," 1982. *Newsweek* May 17, p.105.

Bruce, J. D. and H. Rodman. 1975. "Black-White Marriages in the United States: A Review of the Empirical Literature," in I. R. Stuart and L. E. Abt (eds.) *Interracial Marriage: Expectations and Realities*. New York: Grossman Publishers.

Du Bois, W.E.B. 1897. *The Philadelphia Negro: A Social Study*. New York: Schocken.

Franklin, J. H. 1980. *From Slavery to Freedom: A History of Negro Americans*. New York: Alfred Knopf.

Heer, D. M. 1966. "Negro-White Marriage in the United States," *Journal of Marriage and the Family* 28:262–273.

Jordan, W. D. 1968. *White Over Black: American Attitudes Toward the Negro 1550–1812*. Chapel Hill, NC: University of North Carolina Press.

Lynn, M. A. 1967. "Interracial Marriages in Washington, D.C.," *Journal of Negro Education* 36(4):428–433.

Mangum, C. S. 1940. *The Legal Status of the Negro*. Chapel Hill, NC: University of North Carolina Press.

Monahan, T. P. 1976. "An Overview of Statistics on Interracial Marriages in the United States," *Journal of Marriage and Family* 38.

——. 1970. "Are Interracial Marriages Really Less Stable?" *Social Forces* 48.

Morgan, E. S. 1975. *American Slavery, American Freedom: The Ordeal of Colonial Virginia*. New York: Norton.

Myrdal, G. 1944. *An American Dilemma*. New York: The Free Press.

Reuter, E. B. 1931. *Race Mixture: Studies in Intermarriage and Miscegenation*. New York: McGraw-Hill.

——. 1918. *The Mulatto in the United States*. Boston, MA: R. G. Badger.

Roberts, R. E. 1994. "Black-White Inter-marriage in the United States," in W. R. Johnson and D. M. Warren (eds.) *Inside the Mixed Marriage*, Lanham, MD: University Press of America.

——. 1940. "Negro-White Intermarriage: A Study of Social Control," Unpublished M.A. thesis, University of Chicago.

Sickels, R. J. 1972. *Race, Marriage and the Law*. Albuquerque: University of New Mexico Press.

Spickard, P. R. 1989. *Mixed Blood: Intermarriage and Ethnic Identity in Twentieth-Century America*. Madison, WI: University of Wisconsin Press.

Staples, R. 1992. "Interracial Relationships: A Convergence of Desire and Opportunity," in R. Staples, *The Black Family: Essays and Studies*. Belmont, CA: Wadsworth.

Williamson, J. 1980. *New People: Miscegenation and Mulattoes in the United States*. New York: Free Press.

Wirth, L. and H. Goldhamer. 1944. "The Hybrid and the Problem of Miscegenation," in O. Klineberg, *Characteristics of the American Negro*. New York: Harper.

Woodson, C. G. 1918. "The Beginnings of Miscegenation of Whites and Blacks," *JNH* 3: 335–353.

Wright, L. 1994. "One Drop of Blood," *The New Yorker* July 24, p.1.

Chapter 3

The Couples

As was mentioned, the number of Black/White couples in this country is increasing and much of the research consists of examining Census data (Besharov and Sullivan 1996). A few studies have employed qualitative methods, but for the most part, our understanding of the couples themselves is limited. To really examine the issues and problems interracial couples face, it is necessary to provide a bit of background on the couples themselves.

THE CAST OF DISTINCTION

As Table 3.1 shows, of the 28 couples we interviewed only two consisted of African American wives and White husbands. Consequently, such a small number of this type of interracial couple makes it difficult to draw any meaningful conclusions. This table simply allows the reader a more organized sense of the main characteristics of our population. The overwhelming majority, 93%, were made up of African American

Table 3.1
Profile of Couples

Type	Mean Age	Length of Marriage (in years)	Education (in years)
Black hus./ White wife (N=26)	36.5/34.6	6.4	13.9
White hus./ Black wife (N=2)	37.0/35.0	12	14.5
Overall	36.7/34.8	6.8	13.9

husbands and White wives, which is consistent with the literature (see for instance Besharov and Sullivan 1996; Billingsley 1992).

The overall average age of the husbands was 36.7 years old. For African American husbands, the average age was 36.5, for White husbands, it was 37.0 years old. For White wives, the youngest of the group, the average age was 34.6 years. African American wives were an average age of 35.0 years old. The youngest spouse we interviewed was an African American husband who was 20 years old and the oldest one was 54 years old. The youngest White wife we interviewed was 21 years old and the oldest was 54 as well. The average length of marriage for all couples was 6.86 years, with a range between one and 14 years. Most of the couples dated an average of three years before deciding to get married—this runs counter to conventional thought which contends the courtship is typically brief and the marriage is based on a rash decision (see for instance Mills 1996).

With these couples, at least, the decision was actually one in which a considerable amount of time was invested in the relationship. Moreover, the length of marriage also suggests some stability within the relationship. According to the 1996 *Statistical Abstract in the United States*, in 1990 the median length of marriage in this country was 7.2 years. The couples we interviewed were married somewhat less time than that, but by only a matter of three and a half months.

There was also considerable variation in terms of educational background. We interviewed couples with graduate degrees, including one with a Ph.D., and some with only a high school education. Generally speaking, however, the couples tended to have similar educational backgrounds; if one had obtained a college degree, the other had either done the same or was working towards its completion. Those that had not gone to college tended to marry someone with similar educational experiences. This, too, is consistent with some evidence in the marriage and family literature—most people marry someone of similar educational, religious, and social class backgrounds (see for instance Kornblum and Smith 1996). The average number of years of education for all couples was 13.96. Men tended to have slightly more education than women, with averages of 14.14 and 13.78 years respectively. Not surprisingly, educational experiences translated into occupational opportunities. The employment situations of the wives included homemakers, secretaries, and security guards. There were a few notable exceptions, such as those women who were mortgage managers at banks or were self-employed, but for the most part, they were confined to jobs in some of the lowest paying sectors of the economy.

The men's jobs ranged considerably as well. Some said they were self-employed, while most were teachers, store managers, musicians, telemarketing salesmen, or police officers. There were also a number of cases in which the male was the sole breadwinner and 6 of the 28 families had stay-at-home mothers. Given all this, not surprisingly none of the couples we interviewed felt they were financially secure.

Many of these characteristics suggest that even in a somewhat unique type of relationship, a number of traditional values about family life remain. For instance, one White wife stated, "When we got married and started raising a family, I felt it was important to be at home all the time. That is what most people do and it is the right thing to do." Obviously, the research on the percentage of households where both spouses work has risen considerably since the 1940s and, according to the *Statistical Abstract in the United States* as of 1995 it is currently 61.1%. However, an important note is the perception it is not only appropriate for these mothers to stay at home, but also expected and there is no debating the issue.

Some people might interpret these attitudes and behaviors as an interracial couples' attempt to normalize their family situation, but it seems clear this is not the primary reason. While some couples may use this technique to appear they are just like other families, a more telling insight is that they remain bound to the larger community and attempt to live up to its standards for new parents.

Of those that had children, the structure of the family was also similar to many Americans. The average number of children was 1.6 children per family, most of whom were from their present marriage. This was a bit smaller than the general American trend in terms of family size, but not substantially different. According to the *Statistical Abstract of the United States*, in 1995 the average number of children per family was 2.18 (note: this figure consists of married couple families with their own children under the age of 18). There were a few cases of blended families, which include children from one (or both) spouse's previous marriage who were incorporated into their present situation. This also raises the issue of the spouse's involvement in other interracial relationships.

About three-fourths of the couples we interviewed had been involved in previous interracial relationships. This included other African Americans as well as those from other races, such as Asian Americans or even Hispanics. Clearly, husbands were more involved in interracial relationships than the wives: 71% (20/28) of the husbands had been involved, while only 18% (5/28) of the wives had an interracial relationship prior to marrying their current spouse. A few had been married to someone from another race, but it was most often the case that they simply dated someone from another race prior to marrying their spouse.

Another interesting trend involved service in the military. Over 90% had been involved in some branch of the armed forces. We will have more to say about this in the coming pages, but for now recognize that the military played an important part in the lives of the couples we studied.

A LIMITED CAST OF CHARACTERS

The following descriptions represent some of the interesting contrasts we discovered among the couples. In an effort to protect their privacy, fictitious names, locations (and sometimes occupations) were created. We do this because we feel it is essential to guarantee, as much as possible, anonymity to these families. While there always remains a possibility of discovery by not concealing this information, this particular method ensures their protection.

Sean and Rebecca Sizemore

Sean and Rebecca are musicians in the same band. Sean plays the drums and does background vocals, Rebecca is one of the lead singers.

The band travels quite a bit, although most of their performances occur in the South Carolina/North Carolina area. They have been married for ten years and have a seven-year-old daughter named Carly. Sean is 44 years old and Rebecca is 31. Both graduated from high schools in the upstate area.

The Sizemores live in a mobile home in a rural section of South Carolina. It is a "single wide" trailer, meaning the space is limited. The exterior is a faded white color and at one point in the past someone built a deck/porch by the front entrance. It too is faded and like the entire exterior is in need of a great deal of repair. As I (McNamara) walk up the stairs, the entire structure quivers as if it cannot support my weight. I step to the sides of the stairs, where there is more support from the frame, and step inside.

The interior of the trailer is not much better. The furniture is old and worn, with the foam padding on the cushions pushing through the worn fabric. There is a small television set across from the sofa and perpendicular to the love seat. The shag rug covering the living room is stained and matted down so that it looks like commercial grade carpeting. The kitchen sink is stacked with dirty dishes and the cabinet doors, randomly left open, clearly show there is not a lot of food in this home. While standing in the living room, I catch a glimpse of a bedroom through the doorway on the left. Crossing the threshold is a sleeve from a long sleeved oxford shirt and the cuff from a pair of pants. In short, this home is in a considerable state of disrepair.

Moreover, the smells from leftover fried food and cigarettes linger in the air and the poor lighting inside the trailer gives the wafting smoke a blue tinge. It reminds me of watching a magic show inside a theater where the performance begins with a cloud of smoke produced by dry ice. This trailer is barely in livable condition. Taking a deep breath and hoping the sofa does not break while I am sitting on it, I begin what is to be a two and one half hour conversation with the Sizemores.

In talking to them, it is clear that while Rebecca is personable and able to speak her mind with both clarity and candor, the dominant personality in this relationship is Sean. He is a very strong-willed individual, quick to take exception to insults or threats of any kind. In this way, he is very different from Rebecca, who is able and willing to put up a fight when necessary, but is not as quick to anger as her husband. She would rather avoid a confrontation than escalate it. To illustrate, consider the following. Rebecca states:

I never really thought about race issues until people started talking about it. Like in high school I think I started hearing about it. But I just didn't care. That stuff didn't matter to me, what other people thought. And I think that's true today, a lot of interracial couples worry so much when they go out that 'He's looking at me,' or 'He's talking about me' and they always assume that. I don't even look for it. If you look for it, you'll find it, even if they are looking at you for whatever reason; they may be looking at you because you got something in your hair or something else. I don't like to think of people as being so mean spirited and try to avoid situations like that if I do find them. Now my husband here, he's a different story all together. Where I will try to be mellow about it and take a laid back attitude, sometimes Sean will find problems and then make them worse.

Sean: That's not true! The difference is that I notice it more than you do and I am more sensitive to it because I am Black and you are not. Yeah, I get angry and sometimes aggressive when people treat us poorly, but don't most people? I'm the sort of person that when I get offended, I want something done to fix it. I have threatened to sue people for their actions, like the time the real estate agent tried to keep us from renting an apartment in a rich section of town where just about everyone was White. I believe that if you let them, people will walk all over you. If they think you can't be screwed around with, then they'll leave you alone and find someone else to mess with. For me, I want people to know that they had better treat me fairly or else I'm not going to let it go. Rebecca and I have had many arguments over what we are teaching Carly. I'm trying to teach her to stand up for herself and to protect my family at the same time. If other people are entitled to privileges and certain things, then I don't think it is right to keep them from me. That's why we have groups and organizations to help keep that from happening . . . so why not use them?

Rebecca: See what I mean? I can't get all worked up over little things, where he gets going and sometimes makes an issue out of a small thing.

Sean: But it isn't a small thing, can't you see that? These little things are examples of the bigger problem in our society. And that is that we are all racist to some degree and need to be made aware of it when we act that way. We also need people to know that they will be held responsible if and when they do that. So by ignoring the little things, we make it harder to solve the big ones. It is hard sometimes and it isn't like we are faced with racism everyday, but I would rather make it an issue now than go back to the way things were just after slavery.

This discussion of racism in society was revealing for several reasons. It shows how sensitive Sean is to these issues, but it is also symbolic of the problems all interracial couples face. While the ways in which they solve problems vary considerably, it is important to recognize people in interracial relationships must be more aware of what they represent to society as well as realizing the problems it creates for them, both in and outside the marriage.

What is interesting about Rebecca's comments is that at one point, she actually tried to assimilate into African American culture and to take on the characteristics of a Black woman.

Sean: When I first met Rebecca she sang like a little black girl. So I asked her why she did that. She said that's what the members of the Black band asked her to sound like. I told her 'Look you got a nice voice. Sing like you normally would sing. Forget about trying to sound like somebody else.' See Rebecca wanted to join the band and the guys were all Black and they didn't want her because she was a woman. They didn't want a woman in the band because she would go back and tell their wives and girlfriends what they were doing with other girls and stuff. So what they would do is every now and then they would let Rebecca do a guest thing to pacify me. She would come in and sing a song we arranged for her so she would sing in her own natural voice. But then she started trying to sound Black so we would keep her.

It may be that she simply wanted the job with the band, or it may be that she wanted to impress Sean. It may also be, though, that she is not as clear about issues relating to race as she would like. Moreover, her involvement and marriage to Sean forces her to confront a host of issues that she may rather ignore.

When I ask them what a typical day is like for them, the Sizemores begin by saying their day does not usually begin until the afternoon. This is due to the late night performances, plus traveling through various states with the band. They usually arrive home around 3 a.m., sometimes later, and wake up around noon. After getting up and eating, the rest of the day is spent getting ready for the next evening's performance. When the band has a night off, which is not often, the couple usually spends time in local bars, listening to other bands, or spending time with friends. It is also clear, both from the odors within the trailer, and the presence of several items casually strewn around the trailer, that drug use is fairly common. Thus, most of the Sizemores' time evolves around their band and their music.

Before I can ask, Rebecca tells me about who takes care of her daughter when they are away. Carly usually stays with a neighbor, who has a child the same age. The two girls are best friends and like spending a lot of time together.

Sydney and Tom Mead

Sydney and Tom are also an example of a couple in which the African American husband clearly dominates the relationship. Tom is a massively built individual, standing six feet two inches and weighing approximately 220 pounds. He is an avid weight lifter/body builder who works for a electronics manufacturer. His wife of only one year, although they lived together for three years previously, is pregnant with Tom's third child, one of which is from a previous interracial relationship with a White woman. Sydney is currently on maternity leave from a department store franchise in one of the local malls.

She dutifully waits for him to come home from work or the gym and appears to dote on his every wish. In our discussions with her about being involved in an interracial relationship, she had no opinions, virtually always deferring to Tom for a response. Other times, she simply would state she did not know or had no opinion one way or the other on an issue.

The Meads currently rent a house in a working class neighborhood. It is a two bedroom bungalow built in the 1940s. The exterior is well maintained, as are the lawn and shrubbery, but the interior is a bit different. Inside the home, the odors from a Chihuahua are very apparent. When we inquire if the dog is a puppy, we learn that she is two years old. We also learn that the dog is not house-trained—explaining the odor.

The furnishings inside the home are contemporary and the simulated black leather sofa and love seat have several cracks and holes which have been covered with black electrical tape. Interestingly, adorning three of the four walls in the living room were enlarged photos of Tom in various clothing. All appeared to be posed photographs and while there were a few photos on the mantle of the children, there was not a single picture of Sydney anywhere in the room. The Mead family includes Tom and Sydney as well as Tom's two other children, Amber, age 11 and Greg, age 14.

Amber is biracial and lives primarily with her mother. She visits her father on alternating weekends and holidays. Greg is from a previous intra-racial relationship and lives with his father and Sydney full-time. He does not have contact with his mother, so Sydney is attempting to fulfill that role. She struggles with the demands of a 14-year-old boy, especially one who challenges her role as his mother. Sydney is also worried about how Greg will adjust once the baby is born. She states:

> Well, I don't know what's going to happen. He's okay with Amber I think because she isn't his real sister. Amber has a different mother and she also doesn't live here. I think they get along okay . . . as much as an 11 year old and a 14 year old can. But he's been hard for me to deal with a lot of the time and I don't know what's going to happen when the baby is born. I won't be able to give him the attention he needs.

This concern over sibling rivalry is a common problem in most families, as are the authority challenges of teenage children. What remains to be seen is how Greg and Amber respond to the child and if race plays a part in that adjustment.

For now, a typical day for this family sees Tom leaving for work well before 7 a.m., while it is Sydney's responsibility to get Greg off to school in the morning and then maintaining the house until Tom comes home, which is often as late as midnight. Sydney admits to moments of loneliness, particularly at night. She also says she grows increasingly worried about being alone at night since she is nearing the final weeks of her pregnancy.

Tom works until 3:30 p.m., sometimes later and then goes to a local gym to work out. Afterward, he can usually be found in a sports bar nearby, where he spends time with his friends. He states he needs to maintain this type of schedule due to the stress he experiences at work.

Pam and Eddie Williams

This couple has been married for nine years and met while attending a university in Nevada. Eddie currently works for a telecommunications company and is also a part-time musician. By his own account he is very quiet, almost shy in his interactions with people. He did not date during his high school years and only sporadically in college. This was not due to a lack of interest in women nor they in him. Rather, he was engrossed in his music and was content to simply "hide in a corner at parties" as he puts it, and play the bass or acoustic guitar. Eddie is a product of a military background, where his father served with distinction in Vietnam. Thus, in addition to a naturally reserved disposition, Eddie wrestled with the frequent relocations and always being the new kid on the block. He describes his situation this way:

> So, it's not like I was into the dating scene—I just didn't have a very active dating life. And I didn't say 'Well I like White women or I like Black women.' I was just one of those weirdos who would sit in the corner with my bass and be in heaven. And throughout my high school years there were a lot times they were all White and I was almost always the only Black guy in the class. That's sometimes hard to deal with, especially if you wanted to date any girl, because she was probably going to be White. I had seen some of the looks the other guys gave me about that and thought, 'This just isn't worth it.' I was fine as long as I stayed away from their women. I'm not what you would call confrontational or anything, I just let it slide most of the time. So all these things together was the main reason I didn't do much dating in school. Then when I got to college, I was still a little hesitant about dating. See, by then I was used to it [not dating]. My mom didn't think I would ever get married and my sister thought I was gay.

In contrast, Pam is very outgoing and very willing to share her opinions with people. While Eddie's family spent most of his childhood traveling from state to state and country to country, Pam's family has remained in Maryland and South Carolina. Her parents live in Charleston while her only sister lives in Greenville. Pam majored in psychology in college, although she began as a music major, which is how she met Eddie.

The Williams family currently lives on the fourth floor of a very large apartment complex. This three bedroom apartment is stylishly furnished and very clean. There is a large stereo and television entertainment center in the living room and the furniture is classic in design and appears to be in good condition. There are two cats and two dogs in this household, but it appears to be a happy kingdom in that there are no battles of territory or for our attention. We learn later that within the building, virtually every tenant has at least one dog and sometimes multiple animals.

Pam is a Fundamentalist Christian and tries to live her life strictly according to the teachings of the Bible. Currently, she does not have a job—she is homeschooling their two children, Janis and James. For a period of time she was manager of an apartment complex, but left after she encountered job discrimination because she was married to a Black. She decided to educate her children at home when she discovered the private school, in which Janis and James were enrolled, was not only inadequate in terms of its religious influence, but the two children were singled out and segregated by teachers and other students for their light skin. In describing this situation, Pam had initially threatened legal action against the school, but ultimately decided it was better to just teach them at home.

Unlike the tall and very thin Eddie, Pam is about five feet tall and, as she describes it, "has not yet lost all the weight she gained when she had James five years ago." She also has a very fair complexion, with auburn hair and green eyes. The physical contrasts between she and Eddie, particularly when she is standing next to him, are striking. Like Eddie, Pam is extremely bright, well read on an array of subjects, and has little trouble expressing her opinions on them. She says,

I have never had a problem telling people my opinions. I am a strong and very proud White woman. And the fact that I have endured so much by being involved in an interracial relationship, I think that gives me the right to express my views. After all, if society wouldn't give us such problems by being married, I wouldn't have to get all riled up about stuff as it relates to race. But I won't tolerate the hegemony that exists with regard the way our society treats minorities. And I simply can't sit back and passively allow people to walk all over anyone just because they happen to be African American or whatever. No sir, I have done my homework and I know what the issues are . . . you may not agree with my position, but I do know quite a bit about a lot of things and I will not sit by and let people spread untruths about other people or other groups. To do so makes me a racist and that I can't tolerate.

Pam goes on to reveal a lot about herself in describing how the two met.

Here's how we met. We met in piano class and he was so shy I enjoyed teasing him. I mean I had walked into this class and I had a shirt that had opened up and there was a gap at my chest. Well it took all he had in him to tell me that my button was undone. I think what solidified our interest in each other was that we were in two bands that traveled in the summer music ministries. So we did that between our sophomore and junior and between our junior and senior years. Actually, I had liked him for a long time and had gotten him fixed up with a good friend of mine so we could be near each other because I wasn't really ready to deal with the interracial part. I wasn't sure about it. Now it's easy, but then, even I was concerned.

Then I realized I had said a prayer and I had my list of what I wanted in a husband and I prayed for that. I don't know where I got that from or how I came up with those characteristics, but if you look at Eddie . . . and I mean you just go down that list and it's incredible.

In trying to explain why she was apprehensive about acting on her feelings for Eddie, Pam offers the influence of her parents and the media, particularly rigid stereotypes about minorities. She says,

I'm so sick of the interracial thing being portrayed in the media as a negative thing. You got the poor White trash and the Black guy you know I'm just sick of that. The media continues to create prejudices that happen in our country now. Even who they focus on as the leaders of the Black community are not necessarily the ones who are really leaders . . . Do you remember the Billy Jack movies? I mean I was always so adamant in my thinking—how could they do that to the Native Americans? Any kind of unjust thing that happens to people, whether it be the color of their skin, religion, or anything like that, I just can't stand it. And my parents aren't any better. They are racists too, but I think they've also learned from the media about what is appropriate and what is not. And in their minds, interracial is inappropriate. They taught me that and I had a hard time getting past it because I didn't want to think my parents were wrong. But I'm glad I did.

Roy and Karen Germaine

This was one of only two couples we interviewed in which the husband was White and the wife was African American. Roy and Karen have been married for 14 years and have two children: Kim, who is 11 years old, and Robert, who is 12. Unlike other couples, particularly those with military backgrounds, Karen has served in the Air Force for nearly 12 years and was only recently discharged. She is currently attending a local community college and working as a security officer, her husband handles most of the child care responsibilities while working part-time at as a maintenance man at an electronics manufacturer. In addition, Roy coaches women's gymnastics for the local junior high school team in his hometown.

Karen hopes to complete her bachelor's degree sometime in the next two years—she currently holds an associate's degree in business. Roy graduated from Georgia State University with a degree in recreational administration. He also holds an associate's degree in nursing and has worked as a licensed practical nurse (LPN).

The couple has traveled extensively due to Karen's military service. They have lived in Iceland, Germany, and Minnesota. They have also recently purchased a home in a quiet working class neighborhood. As they describe it, the houses are close together and the yards are rather small, but there exists a sense of community among the residents that allows the Germaines the opportunity to enjoy a sense of place and privacy. It is indeed a cozy home, with wood paneling in many of the rooms, and dozens of pictures of the children and relatives on the mantel above the fireplace. There are also family photos hanging from the walls, and crayon drawings plus an assortment of "A" papers affixed to the refrigerator with magnets. Piles of computer game cartridges in front of the television suggest the children and their friends spend some time improving their skills at Nintendo.

While we talk over dinner and then again afterward, we are struck by the constant flow of children running in and out of the house. Squeals of delight and argument can be heard in the backyard as the children engage in a host of memory-making games and activities. All told, were it not for the fact that the parents were born into different races, this would be a typical American household. While they struggle to make ends meet and worry about paying for Kim's dance lessons, they say they live among a group of people who face similar problems and there is some comfort in that.

Ron is intelligent though his educational background does not translate into his current job situation. He admits to being overqualified for his job, but feels that since they have only recently moved into this home, with all the adjustments needing to be made socially, it is more important for him to be supportive of his wife's educational needs in addition to making certain he is available for his children. At some point, he says, he would like to either go into recreational therapy full-time or work as a gymnastics instructor. For now, at least, he is content to provide a stable environment for his children and to help his wife finish her degree. By then, he says, "The children may be old enough to be somewhat more self-sufficient. Besides, they'll be teenagers soon, so they won't want to be hanging around their dad all the time."

This is Karen and Roy's first marriage, but not their first interracial relationship. Both had been previously involved with people from different races, although neither one was serious. Karen states,

> When I was in the military I dated a Puerto Rican and also dated a White man as well. It wasn't anything serious, and I really didn't learn much about different cultures. It was only when I met Roy that I started to see what I had been taking for granted was actually very different with other groups.

Roy had this to say about his previous interracial dating experiences:

> I had dated a mixed race girl. She was adopted but her adopted dad was Black and her mother was very pale but had distinct African American features. But as far as who was White or Black in her past, we don't know. Now that you mention it, I don't think I ever really said to myself, 'Well, I'm only going to date Black women or White women.' I really think I see or saw beautiful women and wanted to get to know them better. Now I'll tell you I struck out a lot, but it never really occurred to me that I should hold back simply because a particular woman was African American. All I saw was an incredibly beautiful woman who was bright, and, sometimes, interested in me as well.

Roy and Karen met while the two were attending Georgia State University. Roy states,

Well, we looked at each other for about three months and then we dated for about a month and I went off to Virginia and then about two months later, she came to Virginia for about three months. She was working at a turkey factory on the wrong end of the turkey. She came home one day and said we can either get married and go off and follow the Air Force or you can stay here, but I'm going to leave. And 14 years and two kids later, here we are.

Karen: But that doesn't answer the question of how we met. Actually, it was over a fetal pig in an anatomy class. There was kind of an electricity between us from the beginning. We sat two or three seats away from one another and we would come in every morning and look over and smile at each other and say good morning. Then we had to dissect that stupid pig. I couldn't stand the smell and thought I was going to pass out. I always wondered if that lab instructor paired us up on purpose. Anyway, after we tried to get the smell of formaldehyde off our hands, he asked me to lunch. We went and got two egg rolls and two Heinekens and ate in Piedmont Park. And that's how it all got started . . . oh and a bag of chocolate chip cookies. I never really thought about race because, like I said, I had been involved in interracial relationships before, so I never thought it would be a problem and Roy said he thought the same thing. Now my family, that's a whole other story, but for me, I just saw this beautiful man with great legs and felt something and went with that feeling.

Donna and James Johnson

Donna and James are an older interracial couple, both recently celebrating their 54th birthdays. Both had been married (intra-racially) for nearly 20 years before they began their relationship. The two met in college in Ohio and majored in social work together. They went their separate ways after college, but stayed in touch with each other as their lives took different paths. Donna, who is White, married an aircraft mechanic, and went to graduate school for her M.S.W. degree. The couple did not have any children. James married and had two daughters by an African American woman he met while working as a counselor. He too earned an M.S.W. degree, from a school in Illinois. In what could be characterized as a story from a romance novel, both eventually encountered problems with their respective spouses. Once both marriages failed, Donna moved to North Carolina to live with her ailing father.

James decided to pursue a Ph.D. and unknown to him at the time, chose a school in the same state. It did not take long before the two friends began spending time together, helping each other cope with the pains of their divorces, and ultimately realized they had feelings for one another. Five years later, James completed his degree and found an academic position at a school in South Carolina. Donna moved with him and they married a year later.

The Johnsons currently live in a beautifully furnished home in a quiet suburban neighborhood. As they describe it, most of the people who live there know they are an interracial couple and accept them for who they are, rather than as a racial category. The Johnsons try to live their lives in such a way that does not draw attention to themselves and prefer each other's company in lieu of wide social networks. Donna had this to say:

> I have to admit that there are not a lot of places that are attractive to us. As a social worker I sometimes get interested in an area and say to myself, 'Oh what a funky little place' but then realize that it would be almost impossible for us to go there. In some places, and I know this may come off as snobbish, but I find that the places that are wealthier are much more accepting of us. They are at least civil to us and that's all I really ask anyway. Money is still the same color and if you want some of mine, all I want you to do is to leave me alone and not give me trouble. You can have racist attitudes and even discriminate against other minorities. I don't like that but I'll accept it. What I won't accept are those people who treat you like dirt and then expect you to give them top dollar for their services. Don't get me wrong, I have friends, it is just that a lot of them don't know that I'm married to James. We do wonder how they would react . . . would they be as friendly? Of the two of us, I'm much more social than he is. I go to the Unitarian church and I have met some of the nicest people around through them. James, though, is a self-described Lone Ranger, and is happy to be doing his own thing.

Since both are now in their mid-50s, they say they are content to simply live out the remainder of their lives together as a married couple without drawing attention to the fact that they are from different races. They travel frequently to foreign countries and have no children of their own. They are quietly intelligent people, who spend a great deal of time listening to others, which was a part of their training as social workers. Both are very candid and unafraid in describing the problems they encounter as an interracial couple, but they are not militant in their assertions. They do not, as they say, "scream racism every time something happens and run to the local chapter of the NAACP." Rather, in their own quiet but effective styles, they try to understand and enlighten the uninitiated to the troubles they have seen or experienced first hand.

The newest addition to the family has been a Golden Retriever puppy named Buster. In many ways, if one did not know the age or the race of these two individuals, one might think they are a newly married couple beginning a life together. This is how they describe their lives:

> We sort of live a scholar's life. It is quiet, usually not all that exciting, depending on how you define that term. I enjoy going to school, doing research, teaching classes, and having that exchange of ideas with people. It may not sound like much to most people, but a good day for me is spent poking around the library or spending an afternoon in a bookstore sipping coffee and learning something new. My wife has a state job as a social worker and with that comes a lot of pressure, but for her, the ability to make a difference in the lives of people less fortunate is her sine que non. I don't pretend to think that I can escape from the realities of life: I am confronted by it every day. And this is particularly troublesome given my personal life and situation. Americans are not that tolerant of interracial couples—even my own family rejects my wife and me to some extent. It's just that I have known this woman practically my entire adult life and being with her gives my life meaning and purpose. I know there are some significant costs to having a life like this, but I'm willing to pay them. And if it means we have fewer friends or more superficial relationships with our families, I can accept that. I am happier than I think I have ever been in my life and there is a sense of peacefulness that I never had before. Everything would be perfect if we could be accepted for what we are: two people who love each other, who are best friends, and who are not bad people.

These comments echo a theme that runs through what many other couples have described. What is particularly noteworthy is the emphasis on having few social networks, including family members, as well as a hint of the kinds of obstacles many interracial couples face. We will have more to say on this in a subsequent chapter, where we identify the problems as well as how couples manage these difficulties. For now, however, recognize that what James describes is a statement that has been repeated several times by our couples.

Mary and Brad Stephenson

This is the only other couple which consists of an African American wife and a White husband. Mary and Brad met, like many people, through friends. Mary works as a counselor for a state agency, while Brad works construction and a variety of odd jobs. For the past six years, Mary has juggled the demands of a career, a family, and her education. This year she should complete the requirements for her undergraduate degree. The Stephensons have two children, Leslie and Scott, ages six and three. Brad's job situation has been sporadic which has caused some financial difficulties. As Mary describes it, Brad has a history of employment in which he inevitably gets fired or is asked to resign. The reasons vary, but much of it can be attributed to Brad's inability to adjust to the demands of a job. She says he is stubborn, has his own ideas about how things should be done, and does not understand his inflexibility sometimes leads his supervisors to terminate him. This rigidity has not only caused financial problems due to increasing periods of unemployment, but also manifests itself in parenting skills and in his relationship with his wife. Additionally, this is not his first interracial marriage. According to Mary, his ex-wife, also an African American, left him because she believed this myopic view of the world meant "once he understood something there was no wavering from it." In their case, Brad felt that African American women liked to be submissive while giving the impression of independence. As a result, Brad would typically yell obscenities at his ex-wife and strut around making a host of unreasonable demands. When she asked him to do something, particularly if he was home because he was unemployed, Brad would launch into an angry tirade and belittle her for not being able to do it herself.

In a recent conversation, Mary described this situation and said she thought this same behavior was now being directed at her. Unfortunately, the two children hear and see these episodes on a far too regular basis. Mary states,

At least before there were no children involved. He was only married for three years. And when I met him, I thought he was just in a bad place in his life or he was different now . . . I don't know.

And for a while, especially when the children were born, it was okay. I saw hints of it here and there, but nothing on the scale it is now. Maybe he is jealous of my going back to school—he has a G.E.D. and does not seem at all interested in anything that I'm doing. I come home from class and want to talk about things and he could care less about anything I say. Maybe that's it, maybe he feels insecure about himself. But I can't say that this is a recent thing though. He was exactly like this before I met him.

And now, say if we go out somewhere and there is a problem because we are interracial, forget it. He goes off the deep end and makes a scene, embarrassing himself, the children, and me. I wish I could tell you that our situation is a happy one, but I don't want to lie either. I think part of our problem or problems can be attributed to what normal married people go through: all that history that we bring to relationships and the insecurity stuff. But I think some of it is part of being in an interracial relationship. [Why?] Because it is so hard sometimes. It is tiring to deal with all the stuff when all you really want to do is live like any other couple.

So if you begin to have problems, you don't always know if it is because you can't get along with the person or because other people's attitudes and behavior are dragging you down. I wonder how many interracial couples actually stay married for a long time because of exactly that point. In our situation though, I think part of it is me and a part of it isn't. I mean, being in a relationship like this is tough—and if you aren't careful, the whole process can eat you up. And that's what I think is happening to Brad.

Pam and Steve Tolbert

Pam and Steve have been married for nine years. Steve has been a police officer for approximately 15 years. Prior to starting a family, Pam worked for a bank as a loan officer, employed with the company for approximately 10 years. Since that time, Pam has started her own mail order business, allowing her to work at home. At some point in the future, perhaps when the children are both in school full-time, she would like to return to the banking industry where she was very highly regarded by her peers and supervisors. The Tolberts have two children: a son named Andy, age seven, and a daughter named Ashley, age four. Given the time constraints placed on him by being a police officer, Steve cannot share much of the child care responsibilities. However, while Pam currently takes on the lion's share of the day-to-day activities, there is a conscious effort to spend quality time together as a family. Day trips and visits to the zoo are frequent as are camping and fishing in the warmer months.

The Tolberts live in a suburban residential neighborhood in the upstate area, where they are well known members of the Parent Teachers Association (PTA) as well as in their local church. Pam says:

> I really feel like we are a part of this community sometimes. We bake cookies for the bake sale at school, we try to help out our neighbors, we even try to help our friends at the church. Its a good place to live and I am grateful that the children can grow up with this kind of childhood.

Despite these feelings of belonging, and a husband whose career is to protect his community, the Tolberts are still very concerned about the potential for others to destroy what they have worked so hard to achieve. Steve says:

> I have worked my whole life trying to get to where I am today. I have a house in a nice neighborhood, my kids are healthy, my wife is happy. I should be on top of the world. And just when I think I can relax and enjoy what I have, some idiot calls me up and leaves a racist message on my answering machine, or I get a hate letter from some jerk who threatens to burn a cross on my front lawn. Or we'll go to a restaurant and some woman will make some remark about me and my family. It really isn't a big deal, but it wears on you. And I think, 'Okay, I'm a cop. I can do something about it.' But what can I really do?

Recently, the problems Steve refers to have increased. They have considered selling their home and moving to another neighborhood. They have also become more sensitive to issues related to race than ever before. Pam states that a schoolmate made a joke about Andy's light skin in school, and a fight ensued. For the Tolberts then, much of the peace and serenity they have experienced is being threatened.

Lisa and Jimmy Schramm

The Schramms are newlyweds. Having only recently graduated from law school and married just over a year, Lisa grew up in a traditional southern family near Charleston. Unlike his wife's aristocratic background, which allowed her to ignore many of the emotional reasons for opposing an interracial relationship, Jimmy had many hurdles to overcome before he could allow himself to express his feelings towards Lisa. Initially, the two met through a mutual friend on a blind date. Both were very reluctant to date a stranger, but somehow the mutual friend convinced them it was a good idea. While the two stated there was some sort of "spark" from the beginning, Jimmy had a much more difficult time with the idea of dating a White woman. This is somewhat unusual, but nevertheless, Jimmy confesses that his socialization as a child was the main reason. He says:

> Hey, I'll admit it now. I couldn't tell people why I thought it was wrong, which made me even more confused. But somehow I just knew it was immoral. And over time, I really had a hard time with it. Here was this gorgeous, talented woman who wanted to be with me and I was pushing her away. I'm just glad she didn't give up on me.

The couple now lives in a small apartment. Lisa works for a law firm while Jimmy owns a cleaning supply business. This unlikely pair have talked about starting a family, but both want to make sure they are more secure in their careers first. Both confess to a fear of having people mistreat them and their children. Lisa says:

> Well, yeah, I'm really worried about that. I mean, it is not that we will be any different from other married couples, but the way people treat us now will probably be carried over to how they treat our children. I would be lying if I said that this was not a concern. I just hope we can find a compromise to it. I also want to say that I am concerned about my standing at the firm. After all, there aren't that many women in the firm to begin with and I don't want my relationship with Jimmy to adversely affect my chance to make partner. But what do I do? Keep him in a closet for the next seven years? I just have to believe that people will do the right thing.

These and other comments are very telling about the nature of interracial relationships. In Mary's case, her questions about the stability of interracial marriages has been examined (see for instance Billingsley 1992; Besharov and Sullivan 1996). As was mentioned, Staples

(1992) argues that interracial marriages are significantly less stable than single race families and much less stable than all White marriages. There are obviously a number of reasons for this, most notably, the legacy of racism in our society and the stress that places on the interracial couple.

Another interesting way of studying this issue would be to interview divorced interracial couples to learn more about the factors that led to the dissolution of their marriages. Obviously, finding these individuals would be a tremendously difficult task, but the information gleaned from those discussions would be very valuable. Another issue, which we will attempt to address in this project, is the sense of isolation interracial couples experience. This is particularly true in those cases where the spouses' families reject their relationship. Under normal circumstances, it would be difficult to cope with the sense of isolation from the larger society. It would seem logical in those situations the couple would rely more heavily on family members for support. But what happens if familial support is lacking? One of the questions we will explore in the next chapter is the reaction by each spouse's family and implications. For example, has the family bonded together to overcome this obstacle and become more tightly-knit than before, or has the introduction of a spouse from another race caused fragmentation and internal conflict among the family members? More importantly, what are the consequences for the couple in this type of situation?

REFERENCES

Besharov, D. J. and T. S. Sullivan. 1996. "America Is Experiencing an Unprecedented Increase in Black-White Intermarriage," *The New Democrat* July/August, pp.19–21.

Billingsley, A. 1992. *Climbing Jacob's Ladder*. New York: Simon and Schuster.

Kornblum W. and Smith, C. 1996. *Introduction to Sociology*. New York: Macmillan.

Mills, C. 1996. "Interracial Marriage Is Identical to Same-Race Marriage," in Bonnie Szumski (ed.) *Interracial America: Opposing Viewpoints*, pp. 210–215. San Diego, CA: Greenhaven Press.

Statistical Abstract in the United States. 1995. Washington, D.C.: U.S. Bureau of Census.

Staples, R. 1992. "Black and White: Love and Marriage," in R. Staples, *The Black Family: Essays and Studies*. Belmont, CA: Wadsworth.

Chapter 4

A Family Affair

The literature focusing on the family responses to interracial couples suggests many members react with considerable emotion to the couple's decision to date and subsequently marry (see for instance Tizard and Phoenix 1993; Johnson and Warren 1994; Frankenberg 1993). These emotions range from ostracization to embracing the newest member of the family with warmth and love. The difficulties many couples experience with other members of society suggests a heavy reliance on their respective families for emotional and social support. Problems emerge, however, when the family is opposed to the relationship and does not offer support to the couple.

Perhaps the most common reason given by those that oppose interracial relationships is the deleterious effect it will have on the children of the marriage. In general, one of the major issues for interracial families is identifying, preserving, and explaining the cultural heritage to their children. Researchers have often conjectured that biracial children are at risk for developing a variety of problems, such as those relating to the child's social identity (see for instance Adler 1987;

Brandell 1988; Kerwin et al. 1993). Some researchers contend biracial children should simply identify themselves as African American since society will inevitably place them in that category anyway. Others argue children should accept African American as their identity based on the notion they will likely adopt the norms, attitudes, and beliefs associated with that group (see for instance Sebring 1985). On the other hand, Kerwin et al. (1993) in their study of Black/White biracial children, found that children did not perceive themselves as marginal and demonstrated, as did the adults, strong feelings of sensitivity to the views, values, and culture of both Black and White communities.

Clearly, while much has been learned, many questions remain about the critical issues associated with biracial children. Of those experiencing identity conflicts, Herring (1992) notes five types. First, there are issues surrounding the ambiguity of the child's identity. Is the child African American, White, a combination, what? Typically, racially mixed children will be somewhat ambivalent towards their parents' ethnic or racial backgrounds (see Sebring 1985). However, when a child identifies with a particular parent's heritage, it is usually at the expense of the other's. It is at this point that conflicts emerge.

A second type of conflict relates to the child's feeling of social marginality. As Herring (1992) points out, instead of the basic question being "Who Am I?" the question becomes "Where Do I Fit?" While this is not especially problematic in elementary school, as the child enters high school, where one's identity begins to take a particular shape dating begins, it is easy to see how difficulties can develop for biracial children. Since their physical appearance is different, and their families are considered unusual, many peer groups reject them.

A third type of conflict relates to sexuality. This issue becomes important in older children, particularly those in high school or just beyond. The problem stems from the type of partner the child should select. Since they do not fit into a traditional category, and our attitudes about interracial relationships remain complex, biracial females may feel their choice of sexual partners, and their patterns of sexual behavior, may be limited to minority men. Similarly, biracial males may be leery of White women for fear of rejection (Herring 1992). While this fear may be a common problem for all males in interpersonal relationships, Herring (1992) argues it can be especially troubling for biracial ones. It is important to note that these conflicts may lead children and young adults to perceive their situation as dichotomous: that they must choose one race over the other in terms of their interpersonal relationships.

Moreover, as Gibbs and Huang (1990) point out, these patterns can develop early and translate into perceptions and attitudes as an adult.

Fourth are conflicts relating to separation from the child's parents. This involves the typical distance between adolescents and their parents. The question here is "Who controls my life?" Herring (1992) argues that biracial parents tend to be either overly protective of their children or ambivalent about the race issue. Depending on which approach is taken, the children may become more dependent on their parents or more rebellious. The problem is that these normal adolescent attempts at autonomy usually occur earlier in biracial children, largely due to the way the parents respond to their particular family structure.

Finally, biracial children often experience conflicts relating to their future careers. This conflict centers around their attitudes toward achievement and upward mobility. Here stereotypes about racial and ethnic groups permeate the child's thinking about career choices. While they may not seem significant at an early age, Herring (1992) has found some evidence that these early thoughts about what types of people perform certain types of jobs begin early and can have a long lasting effect on the child's motivation, worldview, and level of determination.

Until this point, we have been describing the issues as they relate to biracial children biologically related to their parents. While little research has been done on this (see for instance Baptiste 1984), identity issues and problems may be exacerbated in what are sometimes referred to as *blended interracial families*: those that involve stepparents (Wardle 1996). The reason it can become problematic for these children is obvious. Here the child has already had an identity established only to have that questioned when their mother or father marries someone from another race. And it can become even more confusing when, say, the new father wishes to adopt the child.

As a way of dealing with many of the issues relating to biracial children, a national interracial movement is occurring. As Wardle (1996) describes it:

> The interracial movement now boasts several national publications, many local newsletters, over sixty local education and affiliation groups, and scholarly seminars. We are also becoming more militant about the need for a category on forms—school, federal, Census Bureau, Head Start, birth certificates—that accurately reflects the racial, national, and ethnic identity of our children; and

we insist our children are Biracial, normal, and potentially very successful. (p.197)

Thus, it seems there is some evidence that biracial children are at risk of experiencing a host of problems relating to identity issues. However, this trend has not been firmly established in the literature. Some contend these problems are different in degree rather than in kind for biracial children. They also contend most children can be expected to experience problems relating to their sense of self, however, it may be that these problems emerge at an earlier age for biracial children than those from conventional families.

In our conversations with couples and their children, the parents are often very protective of their children and the problems they have encountered. A few families have struggled with these issues, but for the most part, these children have been able to make the necessary adjustments and have encountered very few problems with others in school or other social settings. This is not to say problems do not emerge, nor does it suggest all couples are willing to discuss them. Similar to other studies, a host of questions remain unanswered on this issue. While the problems relating to children seem to be relatively minor or are handled in appropriate ways, the same cannot be said for the ways in which each partner's family has responded to their relationship.

TYPES OF FAMILIES

Part of the explanation for the families' reaction, both Black and White, is found in the composition of the family as well as the partner's position within it. There is obviously a great deal of variation in describing different types of families (nuclear, extended, etc.). One can use educational background, occupation, social class, or any of a number of variables. However, in trying to understand how the families of the interracial couples react to the new spouse, we find one important factor in assessing the family members' reaction was the level of integration the partner had within their families. How close the partner felt to his or her family had a lot to do with how and in what way they reacted, in addition to the difficulties the partner experienced in trying to square their decision with the members of their family. Consequently, a very general and broad categorization of the families was necessary.

Although not mutually exhaustive, in our interviews,[1] we developed a three dimensional typology: *the intact/traditional family, the distant family*, and *the fragmented family*. The intact family is one in which both parents were present and the partner was close to both of them and to other members, such as siblings, aunts, uncles, and grandparents. Of the 56 individuals we interviewed (28 couples), 20 describe their families with these characteristics. In many ways, this group represented the traditional American family. As Kathy, a White wife, describes it:

> Growing up, I guess you could say that we had a traditional family. My mother and father have been married almost thirty years. My father worked as a salesman of industrial supplies and my mom stayed at home to raise my two brothers and I. I am the youngest, my older brothers are four and five years older than me. Being the only girl, I think my mother spent a lot more time with me than with my brothers. We had sort of a picture perfect childhood: we would all go to church on Sunday and then have a big dinner in the afternoon. Sometimes my cousins would come over and we would play in the backyard or in the pool. At Thanksgiving we would have just about the whole family over and the house would be full of people. And at Christmas, we would decorate the tree and our parents would let us open one present Christmas Eve, and then we would wake up about five o'clock in the morning the next day and tear open everything under the tree in about five seconds flat. I felt close to my family, and my uncles and aunts all lived nearby so we saw a lot of them too. There were a couple of uncles who lived in Georgia, but they usually made the trip up for the holidays. I used to talk to my mother once a week before I got married and one of my brothers still comes over on Sundays to see the kids.

The distant family is one in which both parents are not usually present, and the partner does not maintain close ties with them or with other family relatives. In most cases, the partner is perceived as the outcast of the family—they are always getting into trouble of some kind and do not conform to the standards set by society or by family traditions. In one sense, the family's perception of the partner may explain the distance he or she feels from the rest of them. Twenty individuals have families with these characteristics. Holly, a White wife describes her relationship with the family in this way:

> My family . . . Well, I can say they are what you might call a stable family. I mean my mother and father are still married and my brothers and sisters still get together for the holidays and stuff.

But I was always, and I really think this is unfair, I was always considered the screw up of the family. I was always doing something that they considered as they put it 'inappropriate.' When I was a teenager that might have been true: I smoked pot and got into a little trouble now and then in school, but that was about it. Oh, and I always resented my family's use of the word 'nigger.' If that makes me the family screw up then I guess I'm guilty. Another thing that happened was that I grew up in a small town. You know how it is, everybody knows everybody's business. Well, I had trouble finding a job because everyone in town thought that I was a troublemaker so they wouldn't hire me. It was only when I left and started a life on my own that I realized that it wasn't me being a screw up as much as it was my family, and my friends and neighbors, thought that I was one. But if you looked at my family from the outside, you'd see a lot of traditional values and a commitment to the family. That is, until it comes to me. It seemed like everything I ever did was wrong or stupid, or I did not plan it well enough. Who I dated, how I spent my money, what jobs I took—all of it. A lot of times my parents would sort of nod, like, 'Well she's screwing up again.' So when I started dating a Black guy, it was just another example of my being stupid or reckless in some way.

Amber had this to say:

I could never live up to my family's expectations. My parents do not think that I will ever amount to anything. I could never do anything right and nothing was ever good enough for them. Even when they got divorced, somehow it was okay for them to do it, but for me, I was the one person in our family who, no matter what I did, would always be looked down on for it.

Finally, the fragmented family consists of families blended either through divorce or death, and there are sometimes stepchildren present. This group experiences perhaps the most difficulty in keeping relationships intact and it was not uncommon to learn that members in this type of family had been married multiple times. Sixteen individuals describe their families as having these characteristics. Doris describes her family in this way:

Well, where do I begin? Let me start by saying that my family is, well to describe it anyway, is messed up. I've got brothers and sisters, stepbrothers and sisters, all kinds of aunts, uncles, and cousins that are my real relatives and then a whole slew of half relatives. My mother and father divorced when I was fourteen and then my mother had a baby from this guy, but she never married him. Then she did it again, and the third time she actually married the guy. My father remarried, got divorced again a year later, and married another woman from Seneca. She had three kids from another marriage and then my father wanted a child of his own. Now they just recently got divorced and my father has his eye on another woman that he says he's going to marry. My little sister is sixteen and she's pregnant with her second child, both of whom have different fathers. My youngest brother, he's seventeen, he thinks his girlfriend is pregnant but he's not sure if it is his or not. See, so we've got a whole mess of confusion around this family. Everybody's either gettin' married, divorced, or havin' a baby. And outside of my parents, the longest anyone has ever been with someone has been seven years, that's me and my husband. We have two kids, but a lot of my family doesn't want to be around them. So see, this is not what you might call a normal family situation.

THE WHITE PARTNER'S FAMILY

As was mentioned, Johnson and Warren (1994) found members of the White partners' immediate families were either hostile or fearful of the interracial relationship. The authors found that many members of a White partner's family tried to conceal the relationship from their friends and neighbors. The explanation for this was a concern on the part of family members about losing their status with Whites who would consider this type of relationship unacceptable. Thus, one explanation for the opposition is a fear of losing or damaging their social standing in relation to others in their community.

Related to this is the consensus of understanding among Whites as to why these types of relationships are unacceptable. Rosenblatt, Karis, and Powell (1995), drawing from the work of Frankenberg (1993), identify five broad categories in which the families of the couples they interviewed opposed interracial relationships, all of which evolve around some type of fear. The first was the overall opposition based on societal or community disapproval. Here family members were against interracial relationships because of the greater community's condemnation of these types of couples.

The second, and related, category of opposition revolves around fear for the general physical well-being of the couple as well as the emotional and social dangers. Essentially what many White family members are concerned about are those individuals who may take their racist attitudes and translate them into overt negative behavior toward the couple and their children.

A third reason for opposing interracial marriages relates to the problems and difficulties the children might encounter. This obviously applies to biological children from the interracial couple, but also to those coming from previous marriages. Specifically, the concern is the ostracization of the children by both races and the damage this may cause to their self-esteem.

Fourth are economic issues. The perception by many Whites is that some people opposed to interracial couples will take exception to them in a variety of ways, such as employers withholding job opportunities or promotions because they married someone from another race. Thus, interracial couples, by this logic, can expect to experience job discrimination and a bleak economic future.

Finally, some White family members contend they are against interracial relationships because African Americans tend to be very clannish and would not tend to interact with their White relatives. Thus, White family members express concerns that they would not have ample opportunities to see their White son or daughter, or the children if the couple decides to start a family. In the present study, we find evidence of each of these reasons. As we describe below, many family members strongly subscribe to these as legitimate reasons to reject interracial couples, even when it is a member of their own family.

Reactions

When family members learned of the couple's decision to marry, there were a number of reactions. Granted, while there are only essentially a few possible responses, what was particularly interesting was the reaction based on the type of family.

Perhaps the most common reaction, especially if the couple had not dated for a long period of time, was shock. The couples dated, on average approximately three years prior to deciding to get married. In some cases, however, the time period was quite short. Sean and Rebecca

Sizemore dated only three months before telling her family they wanted to get married. Rebecca states:

> We knew each other for a while before we realized we had feelings for each other. So when we started dating, it didn't take long for us to figure out that we wanted to spend the rest of our lives together. But when we told our families, they were like, 'Wait, what do you mean? You've only been dating a couple of months . . . don't you want to wait a little while?' Even when we told them how well we knew each other, they still had it in their heads that this was too quick. And maybe there's some truth to that. After all, I'm sure this happens to a lot of couples, not just interracial ones. So maybe their reaction is understandable.

In some ways she is right—the suddenness of the decision would be cause for shock by any family. However, Rebecca and others like her feel the intensity of the shock is affected by one partner being from a different race. Sydney and Tom Mead dated four years before deciding to get married. Still, many family members were shocked at their decision. Sydney states,

> They were like, 'Oh my God they're getting married!' I think they thought that there was never really any threat—that we would just date for a while, we would lose interest and then go on to other people. What they never counted on was this thing Tom and I have was going to last and that they would have to deal with it.

As was mentioned, what is particularly interesting is that the responses to the decision to marry generally varied according to the type of family. In those cases where the White partner was a member of an intact family, one of the most common reactions was fear, both for the individual partner, and for the couple and any children they might have. However, this fear was not usually based on the assumption that the African American partner was incapable of providing for their son or daughter, or would not meet his or her responsibilities as a spouse or parent. Rather, the concern was with the implications and consequences of the decision. Consider the comments of Diane Shelley, who married her African American husband, George, two years ago:

When I told him what I wanted to do, my father gave me a lot of reasons, and he said mostly it was a family wide thing. They said it wasn't because of the color of his skin, that wasn't the main problem. It was the fact that he didn't have a college education. My father said, 'Why should a college educated girl be marrying an uneducated Black man? It just won't work!' But I stood my ground and made them tell me why. My father said, 'Look, I'm not racist, I marched in the 60s. It is just that I am afraid of what might happen to you if you marry this man, economically and socially.' So see it was never about whether my husband was good enough, they were just afraid of what would happen if I married him.

Or consider Pam Tolbert's response. She has been married to Steve, a highway patrol officer, for nine years. When she approached her parents, she discovered:

My father was looking very worried. He took me into the bedroom when we first talked about getting married and said, 'I want you to know what you are getting yourself into. I know you are strong and I know he is strong, but there are a lot of people out there who don't want to see you together.' Then he made me laugh but he was saying he was afraid for me. He said, 'In a way it would be wonderful if you end up fat and ugly because that's what rednecks want to see and think that is the only kind of woman a Black man deserves if she isn't Black too.' He liked Steve a lot, it's just that I don't think he could get over the fear of what a relationship like this would bring . . . so he forced himself not to like him and not give us his blessing with our decision.

Very few intact families were initially supportive of the couple's decision to marry. Of those that were, it was usually based on an understanding of multiculturalism and a belief in their child to make decisions that would result in their happiness. Consider what Doris had to say about her family's reaction:

My parents were great about it. They wanted to make sure I was happy, but they were behind me from the beginning. I think they understand that there may be problems, but they have always helped me and respected my decisions. This is just another one of those. Are they afraid? I think so, but they know this is what I want and are willing to do whatever they can to help me. I don't know how many interracial couples can say they had a lot of support from their families, but I know I have.

While only a few were supportive, an area between support and rejection was to simply accept the situation. This differs from support in that while the families accepted the couple's decision to marry, this did not imply they were in favor of it or would lend the necessary social and emotional support it needed to grow. Roy Germaine had this to say about his family:

> Well, my mother and father told me that they were in my corner about my decision, but I could tell they weren't really that supportive. They said, 'We're not telling you not to because we'll be in support of whatever you do, but I just want you to think about your decision.' What that really meant was 'Yes I have to accept your decision because you are an adult and I have no choice over who you choose to marry. But that doesn't mean that I have to like it or think it is the right thing to do.' What it also means is that they are saying they are supportive parents but I knew, and their behavior confirmed it, that they were not going to be a lot of help when things didn't go well for us. They said all those things because they felt that was what they were supposed to say, not because they really felt that way. And sure enough, when we were planning the wedding and other relatives started to give us a hard time about it, where were my parents? They were throwing their hands in the air saying to them 'We know! We know! But what can we do about it?' Thanks Mom and Dad, thanks for giving me enough credit to make choices for myself.

In a few cases, family members had no choice but to accept the situation since the couple were expecting a child. Pam Williams has this to say:

> I will say this. I think part of the reason why our parents became so adamant is because I had gotten pregnant before we had gotten married. Not by choice, but we had wanted to get married at a certain time and, well, in the months that we were planning, I had got pregnant. It wasn't like the kiss of death or anything since we knew we were going to be married and we knew we wanted to start a family. But my family didn't see it that way. And

to some extent I understand, because there were a lot of high expectations for us because we were at a very crucial point in our lives. Part of it was that our parents were surprised that we were even thinking about getting married, but their reaction really shocked us. We thought they would be more supportive in general, but the pregnancy opened up things we were not expecting.

There were a couple of instances in which it seemed a family member opposed the relationship, but did so out of loyalty to another member. As the couples describe it, it seemed as though this happened more often with parents than other relatives. Consider Gina's response:

Well, when I told my parents, they both looked kind of shocked and then my father sort of blew up. He was yelling and screaming and told me that I had just thrown my life away and was I happy about that. But the whole time, I didn't hear my mother say anything against us. Later, after my father went to bed, she came up to me and told me that while she couldn't go against my father's wishes, she just wanted to make sure that I was happy. After a while, even though my father wouldn't speak to me, and even though I couldn't talk to my mother about any of the problems we were having, I sort of knew she wasn't against it.

While fear and shock were perhaps the two most common responses within intact families, this fear sometimes manifested itself in outright hostility. In short, many family members were afraid and did not know how to handle the situation. Donna Johnson had this to say about that:

My father had an enormous problem with it. In fact, one of the reasons we didn't live together is that I was having a very good relationship with my father at the time and I did not want to damage that. My cousins also advised me not to tell him because they thought he wouldn't know how to handle it. Within a month after that, I moved to Atlanta to be with James. It's just something I felt I had to do. It took a long time, but eventually I got my father to talk to James over the phone. He never asked about the race thing and I think on personality and general interests they would have gotten along really well. But my father never gave him the chance. He talked to him on the phone as a favor to me, but I don't think my father could've gotten beyond color, I really don't. But I don't think it is because my father is a racist, because I don't think he is. I think he was opposed to it mostly out of fear. He just wasn't able to handle something like this. It was beyond the realm of possibilities for him to comprehend. So he reacted the only way he knew how—by getting angry and rejecting the idea completely.

Distant family members did not express much surprise over the couple's decision, even if it was unexpected. The most common reaction was a mixture of disappointment and knowingly accepting the situation as if they expected it to occur. A good example of this is described by Lisa Monroe, a waitress at a local diner who married her husband Ken approximately five years ago. She states:

> As far as anybody on my side of the family, I know there was some mixin' but won't nobody tell you. My dad's side of the family used to own most of Pickens County but the Erikson family, my maiden name, they was some hellions. They drank, gambled, ran around with the women and they lost it all. They used to own slaves. I'm not proud of it but I know this for a fact. But when I met Ken all I heard from my family was 'All White women who date Black men are little whores.' That was the first thing out of my brother's mouth. My sister goes, 'Oh that tramp. She's dating a Black guy and she done had a baby.' And my father goes, 'You are a fool, I thought I taught you better.' It was like my parents were so disappointed in me rather than being mad. Like I let them down again or somethin'. Now I will tell you that I was never saintly growin' up. I partied and drank and used to cuss like a sailor and my parents disowned me for about six months because they couldn't handle me anymore. It hurt them so bad to see me let others use me. I guess my dating and marrying a Black man was just another example of my bein' a troublemaker.

Mary Stephenson is currently pregnant with her husband Brad's third child, each by a different woman, and describes the reaction of her parents when she told them about the marriage. She states:

> Oh Lord, when I told my parents about marryin' Brad, it was like they had had it with me. I remember my father tellin' me, 'Mary, what the hell is wrong with you? Can't you make a good decision for once in your life? From the time you were fourteen years old it's

been one thing after another.' He went on rantin' and ravin' for another half hour about how I am no good and I'll never amount to nothin'. If I hadn't been listenin' to it for so long it might have hurt my feelings. But by now I'm used to it. They think I'm the loser of the family. My mother, bless her heart, tried to make it sound nicer, but she was saying the same thing. She said that marrying a Black guy, especially one who has had several children from different women, would be a bad career move. How is who I am going to marry is going to make a difference in what job I get? No, it's just their way of saying this is another mistake I'm making.

A few distant families tried to be supportive of the relationship, particularly if the decision to marry was based on the daughter being pregnant, but it usually was a superficial attempt at best. Lisa Schramm, who has been married for a little over a year, describes her situation with her family:

We were sort of living together for a while and then I got pregnant. It wasn't a big deal to us because we knew we were going to get married. But when I told my parents, there was like this silence on the other end of the phone. Then they said, 'Well, we just want what is best for you. And is there anything we can do to help?' It was so phony. I could tell they were just going through the motions and doing what is socially acceptable. They never accepted Jimmy in the first place and now that we are having a baby, they know they are stuck with him for a while. But they still love me so they have to give the impression that they will help us. Jimmy could die tomorrow and I know they wouldn't give it a second thought other than to be happy that I'm out of this marriage. And now with the baby coming, they have to be more involved because the baby didn't choose his parents or his grandparents for that matter.

The reactions of the fragmented family were particularly noteworthy. Recall that this type of family consisted of a variety of members and a host of unusual situations. One would think the people participating in relationships like these would be more sympathetic to unorthodox circumstances or unusual situations. One might also think that these family members are not in a position to judge others, hence a greater level of open-mindedness. However, this group tended to react to the decision to marry with the greatest level of hostility. Perhaps this was out of concern for the White partner; they did not want this couple to experience the same or similar problems that they had endured. In some ways, there may be some truth to this explanation, as evidenced by Greg Todd's thoughts:

> I think my parents wanted something better from me. I was sort of the family hero. I was the one who was going to make it. I love my dad and I remember standing in the kitchen in my apartment and my dad called me in and said I know about Vanessa. Fear came over me because I didn't know what his reaction would be. I didn't want to be hurt by my dad. I knew he loved me but he's six foot four and weighs 360 pounds. And he is intimidating. He told me he didn't like the idea of marrying a Black woman and that he always hoped that I would do better than everyone in my family. I just did my own thing. I was working on my own and keepin' myself up. I couldn't pay attention to what everybody else thought because everybody else has their own opinions. Everybody don't see the things the way you see them and that's what made it hard for my parents.

Another explanation could relate to social class position. By the couples' accounts, the fragmented family as a group represented the least educated, having little or no understanding of multiculturalism, and the attitudes towards any minority, particularly African Americans, were clearly racist in their orientation. Pam Tolbert offers this assessment:

> I had this redneck cousin that used to work at Red Lobster and he said, 'Pammy, you sure are pretty why are you dating Black men?' I said, 'So what are you saying, Black guys don't deserve pretty women?' He said, 'Yeah, but you could have anybody you wanted.' I said, 'Well, I have who I want and it just so happens that his skin color is Black.' That is a typical redneck thing. My ex-husband is a racist. He would say things to me and he has turned one of my two children totally against me and I just hope my son doesn't turn out to be a racist. My ex supposedly went out and had a petition signed that if I married Steve I would not be able to see my kids. I am so embarrassed to even be known that I was ever married to him. I just wish I had never met him.

Whatever its source, there can be no discounting the intensity of opposition these family members felt toward their African American in-law. However, interspersed with the hostility was a healthy dose of fear, both on the part of the families and the African American partner. Mary Stephenson says:

> Race wasn't really an issue for either one of us, but for me, I did not want to meet his family at first. I didn't have any problem with his dad's house because I knew my parents wouldn't care, but I didn't know what his parents were going to be like. So the issue wasn't about race but it was about meeting his family and when it got to the point when he introduced me to his mother and all that stuff, I didn't want to get that look that I had seen before in other people's moms and dads. That was an issue for me. I was afraid of what they might think.

Thus, there may have been some very selfish reasons why the couple was not accepted by their families. The angry response by many relatives of the fragmented family may have been fueled by the fear of accepting a minority into the family, which, in turn, would affect their social standing with *their* friends and associates. Interestingly, we only found a few instances in which a fragmented family supported or even accepted the interracial couple. There was one instance in which a few family members accepted the situation, but they did so with great reluctance. Karen Germaine says that:

> Of the few people in my family that did accept it, and we are talking about my brother and *maybe* a cousin, but that's it. They did so out of respect for me, saying stuff like 'Well, we just want whatever it takes to make you happy. But I can't come out and say it publicly 'cause you know that'll start a major ruckus.' So even those that did accept it, they weren't crazy about it in the first place and they weren't able to give us much support even when they did.

SUBSEQUENT REACTIONS

Over time, however, perhaps due to the longevity of the relationship, intact families showed a reluctant acceptance of their newest member. The literature suggests this is a fairly common reaction (see for instance, Kouri and Lasswell 1993; Tizard and Phoenix 1993). Russell Kenney, an African American who had a stormy relationship with his in-laws in the beginning, had this to say:

Her mom was still having a problem with it at the time (when we first got married) and was *really* nasty to me, but with her, it's really what looks good that matters—what it looks like to the neighbors and stuff. She had only gotten to meet me twice before because she lived out of town. And she really got difficult when the baby was born. That's when I put her in her place about our relationship. But as time went on, we've been married about ten years now, her mother started talking about my softball games and how I get respect and such. I think she learned a lot more about me as a person rather than as an African American man. She learned that I'm a real nice guy and that if somebody says or does the wrong thing, I will give it right back to them—I can be just as nasty as the next guy. But at the same time, I think she learned something that day. She was genuinely surprised that a Black man could be so nice—that's what she said. She even went to the cash register and tried to pay for breakfast that day. I said, 'No, no, I'll pay for it. Later my wife said, 'You mean she let a Black guy pay for her breakfast?' We had a nice conversation. She's never apologized for what she's done to me and I still don't think she accepts me completely, but let's just say we both know where we stand and it isn't as far apart as it used to be.

In other cases, it appears the fear and concern about the relationship had to do with a lack of understanding of the cultural differences between the two groups. Through increased contact with the African American partner, many White family members realized many of their concerns were based on stereotypical images rather than factual information. Pam Tolbert had this to say:

My mother told me this one time. She said, 'I knew Pam was different because I would go in one room and her other sister would be watching *American Bandstand* and [Pam] would be watching *Soul Train* in another room.' Somehow that meant that Black people are so different from Whites. If my mother was paying attention she would have seen that there were White people on *Soul Train* and Black people on *American Bandstand*. People have these images that Blacks are so different from the rest of us. In some ways they are, but they aren't that different at all. They are people just like you and me. If there is a difference it is based on what we did to them when we brought them into this country. I think people use stereotypes when they don't have any contact with a group of people and they know nothing about them. The problem is that many of those stereotypes are wrong and it changes the way we deal with each other.

Or consider Pam Williams's insights into how stereotypes are constructed:

I'm so sick of the interracial thing being portrayed media-wise as a negative thing. You got the poor White trash female getting together with a Black guy, you know I'm just sick of that. Or the idea that Black men want to improve their status by being with a White woman. The media continues to create prejudices that happen in our country now. Even who they focus on as the leaders of the Black community is bogus.

Related to this was evidence that the African American partner was in fact a loving and committed spouse. In many cases, the parents' concern about the marriage was assuaged by witnessing the interaction between the couple and, as one wife put it, "my father saw that not only was my husband an okay guy, but that he was taking care of his daughter. That made a huge difference in terms of him, and everybody else, coming around."

In those cases where hostilities abated somewhat between the couple and their White families, the underlying reason seems to be the introduction of children. It is as though family members view pregnancy as a sign of maturity and a stabilizing event that allows them to look at the wife in a different light. Roy Germaine had this to say:

I was what you might call a troublemaker and in many ways I think my family considers me the one who has not lived up to his potential. Yeah, I got my degree and stuff, but I don't have a career in the traditional sense and it just seemed for a long time that I was a disappointment in their eyes. And then when we got married, it was just another mistake in a long line of errors. But when the children were born, especially Kim, since she was the first, some of those attitudes started to change. That I had somehow matured as an individual and that by having a child with my wife, the mere act of procreating, I was somehow less of a screw up. I can't explain it, but they treated me differently, as if I had made some monumental stride forward. It was really weird, it was as if all my behavior up to that point was a result of being immature and all my future behavior was going to be more constructive since I now have a child. At some level, too, they also became more accepting of my marriage and more cordial towards Karen.

As was the case with intact families, for those members of distant families that did not initially accept the African American spouse into the family, the length of time the couple remained married had a tempering effect of emotions. The longer the couple remained married, the greater the likelihood members were to accept or tolerate him.

Similarly, time played a crucial element in fragmented families, but perhaps most important was contact with their African American in-law. While a large number of fragmented families refused to develop even the most perfunctory relationships with the couple, preferring instead to ostracize them, of those that made an effort to repair the emotional damage done by their initial reaction, most came to understand and, in a few cases, even respect the African American partner. Brendon, an African American whose marriage to Sharon, his White wife, caused considerable strife within his own family, had this to say about his wife's family:

I have to admit when I first met Sharon's family, I thought that they were all messed up. Who was married for the fifth time, who had children by how many people, and everybody just seemed to be doing their own thing. Nobody seemed to care that much about what everyone else was doing—there was no real family. So I figured that I was covered and that Sharon's family wouldn't care if she dated or married a Black guy. Wrong. They went crazy, talkin' about how it is immoral because of this and it will never work because of that. And that was before they even met me. I was like, 'Who are you people?' With all the stuff they were doing, they didn't have any right to be tellin' us what we should be doin'. And Sharon said so. Well, they must of realized that they were being mean and hypocrites about all of it, so they tried to make nice. I was surprised, especially after all the nasty things they said about me and about Black people. After a while, this is like two or three years, they are like okay with me now. Her father even said that he was wrong about how he saw things from a distance and it took a lot of guts for me to stand up to all of them and make them listen to us. Now they still come to me with these race questions, as if I know everything about why some Black people act like they do, but they do it in a way that I know it's because they want to understand rather than bein' racist about it.

Finally, the declining health of a relative (or of one of the partners) plays a significant role in accepting the relationship irrespective of the type of family. This is obviously linked to the need to settle one's differences when a person suffers from a terminal illness—a part of getting one's affairs in order. James Johnson had this to say:

My father was absolutely against my marrying a White woman. He said I was a traitor to my race and that I was not giving Black women a chance at a wonderful life. He would not talk to Donna, would not see her under any circumstances, and we did not speak to each other for over five years. Then he contracted lung cancer and he gradually became more sensitive to the issues and accepted us. Not with open arms at first, but later, and just before he died, he apologized to Donna and said he was sorry that he treated her so poorly. I think him getting sick was what did it.

Overall, then, what we find is that most of the White partner's families rejected the couple when they decided to get married and even after the wedding took place. While the couple found a few individual members supportive of their relationship, most of the families, whether due to fear, apprehension, a lack of understanding, or outright racism, failed to adequately support the couple in their marriage. This is true even after a period of time passed, whereby relatives remain tolerant but few actually support or embrace the couple.

Among African American families, while there is a noticeable departure from this pattern, there remains some of the same fears and hostilities as experienced with the White partner's family. As Tables 4.1 and 4.2 show, there are almost twice as many intact families among the White partners, but an almost identical number of distant and fragmented families.

AFRICAN AMERICAN FAMILIES

As was mentioned, the structure of the African American family differs from the White family (Staples 1992). Consequently, one might

Table 4.1
Typology of White Families' Responses to Interracial Couples

Reaction	Type of Family		
	Intact	Distant	Fragmented
Support	3	1	1
Acceptance	2	0	1
Rejection/Fear	6	7	3
Hostility	3	1	5
TOTAL:	14	9	10

Table 4.2
Typology of African American Families' Responses to Interracial Couples

Reaction	Type of Family		
	Intact	Distant	Fragmented
Support	2	1	1
Acceptance	4	6	7
Rejection/Fear	0	0	0
Hostility	1	1	0
TOTAL:	7	8	8

expect the reactions to the interracial couple to vary accordingly. For the most part, this was true. In general, the African American partners' families were initially much more accepting of the couple than the White families. This is especially true in those cases where other members had been or were currently involved in interracial or intercultural relationships. In the families we studied, there seemed to be a much greater frequency of African American family members being involved with Whites (typically African American men with White women). Thus, when our couples publicly announced their relationship to the African American partner's family, there was a noticeable absence of the emotional shock. This is true even among African American families that could be classified as intact. Mary Stephenson describes her family and their reaction:

> When Brad and I said we were getting married, my family was like, 'Whatever.' No bombs went off, it almost seemed like they didn't even care. I mean I know they did, but it wasn't a big deal. Other couples we have talked to say their family was in shock or they went crazy, but really, for us, it went off without a problem.

At times, the couples disagree on the differences between Black and White families. Brad adds this comment to describe his African American in-laws:

> We usually try to make the distinction that this isn't automatically the way we do things. It's been used a couple of times with me when I've gotten on the phone and talked with members of her family: 'Well that's just the way the Black family is.' And I make a strong point of that's not the way the Black family is—that's the way your family is.

Mary states:

> But it's so different in the Black and White family. My family we were always kind of close and always helped each other out. So when they could call and ask for money it was like, 'Hey buy what you need.' But with Ron, it's like 'What are you doing?' I said, 'Well this is my family.' And he said, 'No I am your family, we're your family.' And I would have to take a double take on what he was

saying so now it's so hard to break from family when they call and need something.

While African Americans are not as shocked by the presence of an interracial couple in the family, the actual support of the couple is less common. Most simply accept the situation. However, there are some cases of support. Adam Bruce, an African American who married his wife Amber eight years ago, says:

> I would say that of all the interracial couples we know and talk to, which aren't all that many, but a good number of them, they would say that most of the Black families accept their relationship, but aren't really that supportive. What I mean to say is, they are okay with it in that most of them don't start screamin' and yellin' when they hear their son or daughter is marrying a White person. But they don't seem to go out of their way to help either.
>
> In our case though, my family sat me down and asked me if I had thought this out and if it was really what I wanted. When I told them Amber was the best thing that ever happened to me and that I loved her with all my heart, they looked me straight in the eye and said, 'Okay. That's good enough for us.' And from that day on, Amber has been like a member of the family. They invite her over for dinner all the time, they call her about once a week just to talk, and when things go wrong, she feels comfortable calling them and asking their advice. Now there are some uncles and aunts who don't approve of our marriage, and this usually comes out during the holidays or when the whole family gets together. But I'll tell you, they are the first ones to jump all over them and tell my aunts and uncles, and anybody else who says something, they are out of line. I know this is probably unusual, but they just love Amber to death and honestly and truly don't look at what color she is.

In some cases, the racist attitudes many Whites hold toward African Americans are expressed by Blacks toward their White in-laws. In these cases, it seems, the feelings of hostility are not so much focused on the couple, although in some cases they are true, but rather seem to be based on the frustration and resentment of the treatment of African Americans in general.

One tempering mechanism to this hostility, however, as with some fragmented White families, is how the couple seems to get along. The more the couple appears to be happy and content, the greater comfort some family members take in knowing their son or daughter is being well treated. This is particularly true in those cases where the relative is an African American female. Donna Johnson says:

> My father was an absolute racist. He hated African Americans, Asians, Hispanics, everybody that was not like him, although he hates African Americans the worst I think. So when I told him that James and I were getting married, it was like a thunderbolt. He was so angry, he didn't come to the wedding, would not speak to either of us for over two years, and would not allow my stepmother to mention our names in his house. Gradually, and I mean very slowly, he began to hear positive things about our relationship. My sisters would mention how well I was doing and then immediately go on to another subject. Or my aunt, who was the only other one who was being supportive in my family, would tell my father what important work James is doing, and then shift to another topic. So over a period of years, the only thing my father ever heard about us were good things. And though he still does not accept our relationship completely, he told my sister that he was glad that James made me happy. You have to understand, that's a huge, huge leap forward in thinking for him. To even acknowledge that we are a couple is one thing, to say that he is essentially okay with the relationship because James makes me happy is . . . I was shocked when I learned that.

Frequent contact with Whites served as a method by which many of the racist stereotypes were demystified. Unfortunately, a vicious cycle develops in that the only way the hostilities can be resolved is through greater contact. Yet the tension that develops early often precludes a willingness to spend time together.

Finally, children do not seem to be the tempering mechanism in African American families that they are in White families. In some cases, in White families, learning that the couple will soon be starting a family brings the members of the extended family closer together. Among those African American families which are hostile to the White partner, the presence of children does not seem to play an important role in reducing those tensions. Consider what Allen, an African American who married Rachel after the two met while vacationing in Europe, has to say:

In the beginning there were some problems of course. My family is very traditional and does not believe in mixing the races. So we had some trouble from Rachel's family as well as my own. Eventually, I was able to convince Rachel's family that they did not have to accept me, but to be happy for her since she is living the kind of life she wishes to live. My family on the other hand, was not so open-minded. In fact, to this day, we cannot visit them because they make both Rachel and I so uncomfortable. When we decided to start a family, I thought my family might be able to put their hostility aside for the sake of the children. I have one brother who is not married, so this was the first grandchild in the family. I thought that they would be happy to have someone to spoil and at least to recognize they cannot blame the child for the situation he or she was born into. But no. My family continues to snub us and is not at all excited about the baby, that is due in three months by the way, nor have they spoken to us more than once since we told them. It is sad really, because at some point I think they will realize what they will be missing and won't be able to get it back. But I really thought grandchildren would bring them around.

Again, remember that in general, the African American family is much more accepting of the interracial couple, but they tend not to be very supportive. Additionally, in those instances where hostility exists, little can be done to ease the tensions between the couple and the family.

Those instances in which both sets of families are brought together almost always bring tension. Examples include holidays, baby showers, or other events in which the two groups are forced to interact with each other. While the number of these occasions are limited, and we did not explore this in any great detail in our discussions with the couples, in those cases when it was mentioned, most of the couples stated they were extremely stressful and often left them emotionally drained. Pam Williams describes it this way:

I couldn't take it. Here I was trying to bring some family unity to the process of our starting a family and nobody cooperated at all. You would think people would be mature enough to act civilly towards each other for a few hours for the sake of their daughter or son. I was so worried an argument would break out that I couldn't enjoy my own shower. It will be a long time before I suggest a family reunion I can tell you that much.

Sydney Mead, who is pregnant and planning a baby shower, is already encountering many of the difficulties Pam Williams alludes to. She says,

> Well, it is very hurtful for me to see these people try to make us feel guilty for inviting the other side of the family. I tried to tell my father, I said, 'Daddy, this baby is as much Tom's as it is mine and I can't simply not invite his family.' And do you know what he said to me? He said, 'Why the hell not? I've got nothin' to say to them N— anyways so why bring them in the first place?' And Tom's son Greg was standing right there at the time. Now how is that supposed to make him feel a part of my family? Thank God there aren't that many times when we will all have to get together.

ASSESSMENT

Judging from the responses described above, as well as some of those we did not include, it seems that the families of the White spouse, particularly the mothers, are much more fearful of the involvement with an African American and tend to reject the relationship outright and from the beginning. Perhaps, as was mentioned, this is due to gender stereotypes, where White men feel the need to protect White women, especially from those behaviors which may tarnish their social standing. These men may also feel women are unable to make informed decisions on their own and make poor ones when given the chance to do so.

It is also reasonable to conclude that the families of the African American partner have a much greater understanding of how to exist in a multicultural society. This is especially true in those families where members have themselves participated in interracial relationships. Unfortunately, we did not interview any members of these extended families, particularly those who had been involved in an interracial relationship. In any event, the fact they generally accepted the couple suggests their experiences with interracial relationships were such that they did not oppose the couple or attempt to terminate the relationship in any way.

In those cases where the African American partner was the first one in the family to participate in an interracial relationship, the reaction was similar to many of the White partner's family, hostility and in some cases disowning them. This response is obviously an extreme one, but it does give us some insight into the intensity of emotions interracial couple brings to each side.

Some of these responses include ostracization, disowning the family member, or simply making the couple feel unwelcome through emotional and verbal hostility. The upshot is that since society does not welcome or accept these types of relationships, there would normally be a greater reliance on their respective families for emotional and social support. Even here, however, the couples do not get the necessary support they need, and continue to feel increasingly isolated from society. These family issues are but some of many problems interracial couples experience. The next chapter explores the variety of problems they encounter from the larger society.

NOTE

1. This categorization is developed for descriptive purposes only. It is not intended to be a substitute for traditional family typologies. Rather, it allows us to decipher the different responses by family members.

REFERENCES

Adler, A. J. 1987. "Children and Biracial Identity," in A. Thomas and J. Grimes (eds.) *Children's Needs: Psychological Perspectives*. Washington, D.C.: National Association of School Psychologists.

Baptiste, D. A. 1984. "Marital and Family Therapy with Racially/Culturally Intermarried Stepfamilies: Issues and Guidelines," *Family Relations* 33:373–380.

Brandell, J. R. 1988. "Treatment of the Biracial Child: Theoretical and Clinical Issues," *Journal of Multicultural Counseling and Development* 16:176–187.

Frankenberg, R. 1993. *White Women, Race Matters: The Social Construction of Whiteness*. Minneapolis, MN: University of Minnesota Press.

Gibbs, J. T. and L. N. Huang (eds.). 1990. *Children of Color*. San Francisco: Jossey-Bass.

Herring, R. D. 1992. "Biracial Children: an Increasing Concern for Elementary and Middle School Counselors," *Elementary School Guidance and Counseling* 27:123–130.

Johnson, W. R. and D. M. Warren (eds.). 1994. *Inside the Mixed Marriage*. Lanham, MD: University Press of America.

Kerwin, C., J. Ponterotto, B. Jackson, and A. Harris. 1993. "Racial Identity in Biracial Children: A Qualitative Investigation,"*Journal of Counseling Psychology* 40(2):221–231.

Kouri, K. M. and M. Lasswell. 1993. Black-white Marriages: Social Change and Intergenerational Mobility," *Marriage and Family Review* 19(3/4):241–255.

Rosenblatt, P. C., T. A. Karis, and R. D. Powell. 1995. *Multiracial Couples*. Thousand Oaks, CA: Sage.

Sebring, D. L. 1985. "Considerations in Counseling Interracial Children," *Journal of Non-White Concerns in Personnel and Guidance* 13:3–9.

Staples, R. 1992. "Black and White: Love and Marriage," in R. Staples, *The Black Family: Essays and Studies*. Belmont, CA: Wadsworth.

Tizard, B. and A. Phoenix. 1993. *Black, White, or Mixed Race? Race and Racism in the Lives of Young People of Mixed Parentage*. New York: Routledge.

Wardle, F. 1996. "Children of Mixed-Race Unions Should be Raised Biracially," in Bonnie Szumski (ed.), *Interracial America: Opposing Viewpoints*, pp. 197–203. San Diego, CA: Greenhaven Press.

Chapter 5

Stepping Over the Line: Problems for Interracial Couples

While the lack of acceptance by family members is serious and causes great distress to the couples, they must confront a host of issues and obstacles on a fairly regular basis. And while some of the behaviors are relatively benign, this does not mean they are not painful. Moreover, some of the problems force couples to take drastic measures to cope with them.

THE PROBLEMS

The literature on the problems interracial couples encounter suggests that their scope and magnitude is fairly wide. Obviously, more extreme or dangerous behaviors are less common, but their impact extends far beyond individual victims. The reason relates to the fear it generates for other couples. This type of fear has been well documented. For instance, a number of studies dealing with the fear of crime have shown it is the psychological harm which makes crime so damaging to nonvictims—it instills the feeling they could be next. This feeling, in turn, alters behavior in such a way that it changes social and emotional networks as well as the overall nature of social interaction (see Seigel 1992; Adler, Mueller, and Laufer 1995).

In a similar way, a number of serious incidents involving interracial couples have received considerable attention from the media, and as a result, other couples are made keenly aware of the possibility of a similar fate. Thus, while it may appear that attacks on interracial couples occur infrequently, the implications are serious and extend far beyond the individual couples.

One of the most common problems experienced by couples are stares by others, particularly in public places. In Minnesota, Welborn (1994) found that 64% of Black/White couples experienced some sort of negative response, the most common of which were stares, compared to only 4% of African American couples and only 7% of European American couples. Similarly, Porterfield (1978) discovered many interracial couples complained of hostile stares by others.

In our interviews, couples complain of a similar problem. Most of the time, the couples' explain this as a form of curiosity. James has this to say:

> Most of the time people are staring at us, but I think it is because they have never seen a couple like this before. So, yeah, they aren't being very polite, but most of the time it is either shock or they are simply curious about it.

Roy offers his insight:

> Well, that's a common problem. In general from people out on the street who don't know you from Adam, that's one thing. If you sit there and think about if somebody is looking at me or at us or our children, that could drive you crazy. Especially since most people aren't trying to be mean about it. They're just wondering about what our story is, that's all. Some of them don't approve, but that's another kind of stare. For these kind though, it's harmless because they aren't saying anything behind it.

What must be remembered is that stares are interpretive gestures and require an assessment on the part of the person receiving them. In fact, at times these gestures can be misinterpreted to convey hostility when none is intended. Consider Eric Williamson's response:

Well, when we lived in Florida it was a small little town and I was
the first Black to live in that area and the kids came to me one
afternoon and said some kid stared at her and thought she called
her a nigger. Being Black, you know, I was angry but then I realized
that I needed to make sure that the kid wasn't just staring. As it
turned out, the kid did stare and then asked my daughter what
race she was. When my daughter said she was biracial, the other
child didn't know what she meant. The kid then asked my daughter
what a nigger was. That's how it got turned around. But it started
by this child staring at my daughter and trying to figure out what
she was. I learned a lot that time about not always being so quick
to react to people. They may be staring and acting for a lot of
reasons and what might be considered a racist remark can get
blown totally out of proportion.

Mary offers this observation:

I have this physical disability that causes my skin to break out in
red blotches at different times of the year. One day I was at K-mart
with my husband and this man walks up to me and asks 'How does
that make you feel?' I'm ready to go off on him and tell him that I
love this man and just because he is Black does not mean I am any
different from any other married woman. He must have seen that
I was getting ready to explode and then looked at my husband and
realized what he said. He goes, 'I'm sorry, I meant your rash—does
it itch or burn because I get one just like it.' So see, sometimes we
get too sensitive about our relationship, especially in public.

While mistakes are sometimes made, interracial couples are forced to
become adept at "reading" the intent of the gestures and comments of
people. As Mary's comments point out, at the very least, couples are
usually quite sensitive to the potential threat or implication of someone
else's behavior.

In the Public Eye

Another problem encountered by couples involves the treatment they
receive from those who work in the service sector of the economy. Waiters
or waitresses at restaurants, gas station attendants, convenience store
clerks, and sales staff in retail outlets, or even other customers at these

places, often make their feelings known. In these cases, the mistreatment ranges from subtle messages to outright hostility. Consider what Holly has to say:

> I know we get discriminated against when we go out to eat. They think we aren't going to leave a good tip. I was in the restaurant business for eleven years. Servers hate to wait on Black people because they always want straws and extra things and leave a dollar tip. We leave good tips and I feel bad leaving a bad tip even if the service was bad because we had been classified as bad tippers because we are interracial.

Lisa Monroe offers this observation:

> So we were going into this Pizza Hut and a couple was following us and it was very obvious that they were out to make our time there uncomfortable. They were very outspoken and they ended up ordering the pizza and then leaving and making a big scene, huffing and puffing and slamming things down. My sister said 'Why don't you say something?' But see, this town is still very good old boy and still have the railroad tracks and Blacks live on one side and the Whites live on the other side.

Consider Jimmy Schramm's response to this question:

> I think one of the biggest problems we have in public are things like being served at restaurants. Sometimes the service stinks or takes too long or sometimes the food is really bad or kept over long. I try to tell my wife not to think about it, because sometimes it is just that—bad service. But it happens often enough for us to think it is more than that.

Russell Kenney has had this happen several times:

> We go into a restaurant, together, with our children. We will order the meal and when we are done, the waitress hands us separate checks. Like she is saying 'There is no way you two could be together.' And here we are sitting with our children, who are obviously fair skinned: who does she think they belong to?

A related problem involves real estate agents. There have been numerous studies conducted on the phenomenon known as "steering" (see for instance Jaret 1995; Yinger 1997). This is the practice used by many real estate agents to discriminate against minorities by selling them property, homes, or renting apartments only in minority neighborhoods. That is, the agent steers the prospective tenant away from the all-White neighborhood into one that is comprised primarily of minorities. Yinger (1997) recently found that housing agents showed fewer housing units to minority customers and provided less help in finding housing that met their needs. He also points to other research that suggests banks and other lenders are much more likely to reject a mortgage by a minority than from an equally qualified white person.

As it relates to interracial couples, Pam and Eric Williamson offer this experience:

> This town has a large number of like-degreed or professionals and most of them do not live in town. We were in an apartment and did not know at that point that we were moving into that side of the road the builder promised the people that there would be no Blacks living in that apartment subdivision. So we get to the real estate office and the agent is really trying to convince us to live in another area. She was saying things like, 'Well, I think you would be happier here, there are a lot of families with children your age, it is closer to work, it is cheaper per square inch, stuff like that. And when we pressed her for the apartment, she put us off for a couple of days and then told us the apartments had been rented to someone else. But, she still had places for us in a primarily all-Black neighborhood.

Sean Sizemore says:

> Oh it happens all the time. You call them up and they'll be nice and everything and take all the information down for you. Then you meet them at the house and you can just see it in their eyes. They want no part of this situation. And I don't think all of them are racists. I think the nature of their job keeps them from lending money or selling property to Black folks. But it is still steering, however you want to define it.

SERIOUS REACTIONS

Some couples are ostracized by their coworkers, or encounter hostility from them. While isolation in the workplace can damage one's sense of self-esteem and morale, much more serious are those instances in which the person is denied promotion or sometimes receives disciplinary action that is racially based. Consider this situation, as described by Amber Bruce:

> We had been dating for a while. I was working at one branch and he was at another. Everyone would ask us if we were dating and we never gave anyone a straight answer. But then I became a floating teller and one Friday my manager told me he wanted to talk to me and asked me to resign and if I didn't resign, they would fire me. I had no idea what could have happened. I had never gotten a bad report before. Then I heard him say there was no way he was going to have someone from an interracial relationship work for him.

Tom Mead's response reflects the problems interracial couples face even if they are self-employed:

> My sister is in the cleaning business and one day she was cleaning this man's house and overheard him on the phone. He was talking to one of his buddies. 'Yeah, the cleaning lady is here but she ain't like other cleaning ladies, she ain't a big ole nigger.' My sister couldn't believe it. He came in the kitchen and asked her if she heard what he told his friend. She just kind of looked at him and didn't say anything, but thinking to herself the whole time, 'I'm glad my brother didn't hear this and I hope he doesn't fire me.'

Pam and Eric talk about their experiences with job discrimination:

> Yeah, our last place where Eric was bypassed for promotions, part of that good old boy system. He was obviously the more qualified person but didn't get it. And for those people who are against affirmative action, my husband was the most qualified, and was Black, and he still didn't get the job.

Adding to his wife's point, Eric states:

There were a lot of things that I saw we were doing wrong and losing money and I think that if the company goes under and I didn't do anything to stop it, then I'll feel bad. So the things that I saw, I made a list out and told my boss I'm giving this to you and I don't want the credit, just take the list and run with them. I did this for several months. Then he finds out that I married a White woman. All of a sudden he was cold toward me and he told me that I was becoming a problem. Then my evaluations weren't as good and I had to leave. But all the things that I suggested he took credit for and got promoted. When I asked him about it, he wouldn't come right out and say it, but I know in my heart it was because I married a White woman.

In describing his experiences on the job, Ken Monroe calls attention to the problems in law enforcement:

I have never had a job that has so much racism as the one I do now. Law enforcement is so bad. That is one thing that if I had to do over again, I would not be a police officer. I have had to hide the fact that I married a White woman because I knew if my supervisors found out, they would make my life a living hell. I shouldn't even be talking to you about this. I know I never said anything the last time I talked to you, but it is a real problem.

Obscene Phone Calls

Unlike work-related problems, where there always remains the question of whether it was due to a lack of adequate performance or racism, in other cases there is no need to interpret the intent of the respondents. Some couples receive obscene phone calls when it is discovered they are involved with someone from another race. Here is what Pam Tolbert has to say:

When we first started dating, a lot of people were up in arms over it. We figured that some people would say a few things about us, but really nothing serious. What we didn't count on was the phone calls. Some people would call at all hours and tell us how Whites and Blacks should never mix and all that kind of stuff. Some of the stuff was so nasty and made me feel so bad, I couldn't get over it.

This went on for about two months and finally we changed our number.

Jimmy Schramm makes this observation:

I think that people who make obscene phone calls are cowards in the first place. They can't say these things to your face—they have to hide behind the telephone to do it. We had a few calls when people found out about our relationship. I figured out who I told and when, and then realized it was someone I thought was a friend of mine. I confronted him and he stopped doing it. But he had already told some of his friends and they started doing it too. We got caller ID and that took care of it. But who wants to deal with that kind of thing in the first place?

Hate Mail

This type of problem is similar to obscene phone calls except there is some tangible reminder of how difficult it is for other people to accept the couple's relationship. A few couples say they receive letters from people who are clearly racist and vehemently oppose interracial relationships. In addition to obscene phone calls, the Kenneys have to deal with hate mail as well. Russell states:

We kept getting this stuff about the Ku Klux Klan and neo-Nazi stuff. Whoever sent it would sometimes include a letter scribbled on it saying something like they were going to burn a cross on our yard or call the local Skinheads and stomp on us. Other times it would just be the papers they printed, like their newsletter. I think it was just to show us they were around and knew we were together.

In other cases, however, the African American partner is singled out for this type of treatment, not because of their relationship with his or her spouse, but because of his or her race. Greg Todd has this to say:

I had a few encounters with some White guys in a bar and they knew some of the people I knew at work. After that, stuff started getting delivered that was racist. You know, cartoons of an African male and a bulls eye circle around it. Or a list of 'What do you do with a dead nigger?' jokes. Stuff like that. These guys, and I know it was them, they never knew I was married to a White woman. But if they did, man, I hate to think what they would have done. I finally had to get a Post Office box because I was sick of dealing with it.

EXTREME REACTIONS

While the aforementioned problems can be distressing and are a source of concern, far more serious are those situations in which people attack the couples or their property. Many of the couples state that vandalism is not at all an uncommon event. In fact, this is usually part of a series of harassments inflicted on them by others. Rebecca Sizemore states:

Well, it started out with stupid phone calls and a mean letter or two. But we just tried to ignore it. That wasn't enough. When they didn't get the response out of us that they wanted, they escalated it. Our car tires got slashed, then somebody put sand in our gas tank. Then somebody decided to spray paint our house with graffiti. Finally, one night we came home from shopping and found every window in our house on the first floor had been smashed. This was in like January and we couldn't get someone to come and fix them until the next day.

Far worse are those instances in which individuals are physically attacked. This is by far the least frequent response, but at the same time, the most dangerous and damaging when it occurs. In a number of cases, these instances occur in traffic. James Johnson has this to say:

I think the worst thing that has ever happened was when we were going to Spartanburg that time. My wife has totally blocked this out of her memory and I remember it like it was yesterday. We were dating and going to Spartanburg and I had my white BMW and we were going up I-85 to get something to eat.

These two guys in a pickup truck pulled up beside us and he looked over and saw us and had his Budweiser you know and they thought they would have some fun at our expense. So when they saw us they started to come over in our lane so I slowed down and they got in front of us and then slowed down to like 25 miles an hour and we had traffic backed up so I went around them in the other lane and sped up and got in front of them.

Well they caught up and got on my bumper. I said 'This is crazy.' They came up beside me and started to get in my lane and I slowed down. So finally, I got back over in the fast lane and as I went by them and they started to come over again. I told Donna to lay down. She said, 'What you gonna do?' I said, 'Just lay down.' I took out my gun and rolled the window down. They were just laughing and looking at each other not looking at me and then when the driver turned around and saw the gun sticking in his face, he lost it and went off the road. All I could see was smoke. So we got back up to 55 and went on about our business. People were pulling up beside us just clapping their hands. They had traffic backed up. I thought that was the worst thing that had ever happened.

Karen Germaine has this to say about her experiences in the car:

In the car, that's where a lot of the problems happen. And then that one time when we were in Nickeltown, that girl we drove by and she said 'Get out of that car bitch! You got no right to be in that car with him.' That's a big thing, especially with Black women and the way they treat Black men.

Adam Bruce offers this insight:

I feel safe most of the time when I'm on the road but there were some really hostile looks, more than staring. I never had cause for concern until about two and a half years ago there was a shooting incident of an interracial couple on the highway. Anyway, ever since then I've been concerned about being the victim of such an incident, so I keep a pistol nearby at all times.

OTHER PROBLEMS

A number of African American husbands state that they are often confronted by African American women who ask them why they are involved with a White woman. In the course of the conversation, the woman implies or openly complains that the husband is abandoning his people, his race, and that he is somehow a traitor for doing so. Brad Stephenson says:

A lot of times we'll get these side comments from people, mostly Black women, who tell me that I am some sort of traitor to my race because I married a White woman. Sometimes it is like mumbling it as they walk by, but other times it is loud and clear. What I don't understand is how I am a traitor to my race when I am still interested in Black issues and the Black culture. I just married the most beautiful woman I had ever seen in my life and she makes me so happy. I am somehow a traitor for being happy? I don't understand.

Eric Williamson states:

I've been a musician in both Germany and the States and how mixed couples get along basically by conversation. White girls are a little more, like if we go to the bar to have a drink or whatever, they will always come and talk to you. Black women will be stuffy as hell. See that's because the Black woman thinks the world owes them something.

Comments like these are a common assertion by African American women and it is not exclusively directed at African American husbands. There are several instances where a White wife recounts a rather caustic conversation with an African American female. At other times, however, the problem comes from African American males. Consider what Karen Germaine has to say:

When we first started dating down in Atlanta, most of the Black males would give me a hard time about me dating him, especially when they would see us together and say 'Well why are you with him? Can't you do any better?' So I guess most of it was from the Black males more than anything, at least with me.

While most of the time the questions of loyalty come from members of the African American population, there are also times when it comes from unusual sources. Pam Williamson says:

One day I took the children to day care and this White woman comes up to me and says, 'Think about what you are doing to those children.' I just looked at her. Then she said, 'Do you have any idea what happens to people when the races start mixing? No self-re-

specting White woman would do that to the White race.' Can you
believe that? And this woman, I later found out, was not some
screaming Ku Klux Klan sympathizer. She just thought that I was
ruining the White race, as well as the lives of my children, by
marrying my husband.

What is interesting is that there are not as many complaints made of
African American women who choose to marry White men. Whereas
African American women publicly condemn their male counterparts for
the loss of their culture, Whites who take exception to other Whites being
involved with Blacks criticize the person on other grounds. As was
mentioned, many Whites raise concerns about the children produced
from interracial marriages.

Although most of the parents were reluctant to discuss the problems
their children encounter as a result of their relationship, feeling as
though they need to protect them, a few were candid about the problems
they experience. When we asked other parents if these problems were
common, most agreed, but were still unwilling to discuss them in any
depth. Most were simply content to state that the children did not
experience any problems. In short, they believe their children are well-
adjusted kids, normal in every sense of the term. While this may have
been the wish of the parents, the fact that they acknowledge the
commonality of problems suggests the realities of being biracial are far
more complex than the parents are willing to reveal.

Of those that did respond, one of the most common problems occurred
in school, particularly in high school. Eric Williamson comments:

> My daughter has had some problems, yes. When she got into Lee
> High School, it was all White and she had some major problems
> there. She'd have notes on her locker that said "Nigger get out of
> here." She was born and raised in Chicago up to nine years ago and
> in Chicago she never had no problems.

One African American woman comments on the problems her teenage
daughter feels about being forced to choose the type of person to date.
She states:

> When I first moved down here I thought I couldn't have a boyfriend
> because of me liking Black men. For the first year I lived here I
> didn't date or anything. And then when my daughter started

dating, she had a real problem—she thought she had to choose one race over the other. As much as I told her she needed to find a guy she liked, never mind the race, I think she felt as though she was disappointing me by dating White guys. It was really hard, especially when I started dating again and her White boyfriends would come over and see me with a Black guy. She never told me but I think she paid the price for that more than I did.

In some cases, the biracial child embraces one race at the expense of the other. Consider Holly's comments:

My daughter is so pro-Black it's sickening. She thinks she's Black—I hate it. What am I, chopped liver? She dwells on this Black thing. So heavy that when her friends come over the house, she doesn't tell them she has a White mother. She lets them think I am the housekeeper. It breaks my heart. It's like I'm nothing. It hurts. Yeah, I'm a White mother but I'm still your mother, I don't care what color I am. She's still a child in many ways and is trying to find out who she is. She only knows herself now as a "Black" person and how White people have treated her in the past. Granted, that wasn't a great experience. White people basically treated her like crap. In high school, they left notes on her locker, spit at her in the halls, and even threw stones at her. So in some ways I can't blame her, but I am not the enemy.

Still another parent talks about how the issue of identity becomes important to many children, even at an early age:

My son came to me one day and asked me why he was so different from his mother. He wanted to know if she had done something wrong and was God punishing her for it by making her look different. Then she wanted to know why her sister looked more like their mother than their father? My two children look very different: one is very dark with common Black features, while my daughter is light skinned and looks like Vanessa Williams. She even has blue eyes. So it was hard to explain to him that different did not mean anything bad, and that he shouldn't feel as though he was singled out or that his sister was either. But I know I didn't explain it well enough and it bothers me that this stuff about who am I and why am I different may make him feel inferior. I guess this is a problem all parents deal with, but it seems to me that biracial children would have a much harder time with it.

This parent's comments are not only insightful, but they are supported by the research on the subject. As was mentioned in the last chapter, the problems of identity are a central theme in the literature on biracial children. And not only do these children experience this problem in somewhat profound ways, they also progress through the typical stages at an earlier age (see for instance Gibbs and Huang 1990).

It is difficult to determine if the stereotypical images of interracial marriages play a role here. Biracial children may experience a number of unique problems. Or, it may be that stereotypical images influence people's reactions when they see the children, which create problems. In other words, is it really the case that biracial children cause problems and conflicts for their families, or do people's concerns that there might be problems for children actually lead to their creation? Does a self-fulfilling prophecy emerge from these conditions? In either case, there can be no doubt that some interracial couples are forced to manage an array of problems that involve their children.

RACISM

In addition to and a central part of the problems described here, most couples have experienced some form of racism during their relationship. Listen to the ways in which the problems have deeply affected them, as couples as well as individuals. Roy Germaine:

> I didn't think racism was an issue. I used to think that all of it was all in the Black people's heads. I didn't think the problems were just becasue they were Black. Then the longer we dated, I don't know if I just noticed more or if it got worse. I don't think it got worse. In becoming more aware, I tried to make my fellow White men more aware, like my sister. I would tell her that this is very real. She said that it was all in their imagination. Well, she is learning the hard way that there are racists and they are very vocal about it when they want to.

Lisa Schramm, a White female says:

It's always the Whites that start the crap. All these guys were doing was trying to go to school. It's always the Whites who somehow feel threatened when Black people start getting what they should have been getting for a long time. When I was in school, I didn't see no Blacks putting notes on White kids' lockers and I didn't see no Blacks wearin' sheets on their heads either.

Roy, a White husband, states:

The racists in this part of the country want to maintain that Deep South thin line. They would rather lose all their business so that they can keep their way of life—that's what's happening. And in some ways, that's not just a White thing, the Blacks are resistant to change too.

Ken, an African American, talks about how his vision of the world has changed as a result of the racism he has experienced:

When I go to a restaurant, I literally check everyone out. I have to, I need to protect my family from the jerks that are out there. We've had trouble in restaurants, in the car driving down the street, in the job, even our families are not that helpful. And I'm sure there are a lot of other interracial couples who experience the same thing we do. So if it has made me a little gun shy, then you're right. And for those that think racism is a thing of the past, they are just simply wrong. It is there every single day. Now what you do about it is something else. It can eat you up or you can find a way to deal with it.

Roy talks about his newfound sensitivity to the racism to which he has been exposed:

Some of the things are kind of hard to define that you know this is happening to us or to someone else because we are Black and White and hopefully, I'm not so shallow that I assume it's because we are Black and White. And some of it goes back to people using the nigger word . . . At work right now the guy I work for says 'Well that old nigger boy but he grew up in South Carolina and has never really been anywhere.' And then there is this huge Black man that is the floor sweeper and says 'You know, I'm the inside nigger and that's the outside nigger.' And I would like to just get him aside and just slap him because there are a lot of us who take great offense and have worked really hard to try to eliminate and do away with some of that and here he is giving license to the stuff that's been going on. And even though he uses the word you can tell that there is not anger or animosity or it's not said with derisiveness. But that doesn't really help because it still hurts.

There are also a number of cases in which African Americans have been exposed to racism but nevertheless continue to be surprised at the ways in which others are so firm in their beliefs. Brad says:

My sister's husband is very aware of racism because he grew up with his father calling Black people niggers. He became a Christian and went to Bob Jones University and his best friend there was a Black guy. He was calling on a customer one time and talking to the guy's secretary and she starts talking to him about a guy he used to work with named Shepherd and said 'Didn't you used to work with that Shepherd guy?' and he said, 'Sure did.' She said, 'Yeah I used to just really like him until I found out.' Chuck said, 'Well, what was that?'And he knew all along that what she was getting at. Shepherd married Sharon and Sharon is Black and Shepherd is White. She said, 'I used to like him until I found that out. I just can't agree with that. You know you don't see the birds and the monkeys together.' And Chuck is just floored.

She said 'You know we are doing the Bible study at my church and I guess God forgot about them.' He said there are only two times in his life that he has been dumbfounded and that was one of them. He said the saddest thing about the whole situation was that the woman really didn't see that as being horrible. I mean the birds and the monkeys, and that for some reason God shouldn't love them. I've heard people say before 'You know, you don't put dogs and cats together,' well, if we cut your skin and don't you bleed red? If you study the human body the only thing that is different between Blacks and Whites is that Blacks have more melanin in their skin, that's all it is. I mean there are some things like hair is different. Some people believe that if you were to have an accident and needed blood and a Black person donated blood, they would have to run tests to see if a Black person donated the blood. Can you believe it? I'm still amazed at that.

Thus, it seems there are a host of problems interracial couples experience. Consequently, it is not surprising to learn many of the couples feel as though they are somewhat suspicious of people in general and are very sensitive to the meaning, both intended and unintended, of the behavior of others. Related to this is that when they appear in public, many couples feel as though they are somehow singled out for attention and have to act differently than they would if they were a "normal" couple. As an illustration, consider Sean Sizemore's response:

> When we go out in public, we feel as though we are on stage for everyone. Not that we are looking for the spotlight or anything, but we just feel very visible and everything we do is being scrutinized. Now this may sound paranoid because I don't think it happens all the time, but it sure feels that way a lot. It also feels as though I am some sort of representative of all the interracial couples, which I'm not. Do you understand what I'm saying?

COPING MECHANISMS

In response to these problems, couples have an array of techniques to manage. While each of these techniques is not used exclusively, they do represent the degree to which couples must adjust and adapt to their standing within the community. In an attempt to gain greater insight into the ways in which the couples adapt to various social problems, Figure 5.1 offers a typology of these coping mechanisms.

Ignore It

One of the most common responses, particularly for minor offenses such as staring, is to simply ignore it as an oversight. Roy states:

> My wife notices that thing more than I do. I go into a place just like you would, not thinking 'Okay there are the White people and the Black people' and even thinking about any of it. If they are staring I don't notice it.

Eric states:

> We have seen a lot of instances where we could have responded, maybe even should have responded, but we just didn't pay any

Figure 5.1
Typology of Respondents to Problems

TYPE	DESCRIPTION
Educators	Attempts to help people understand and accept interracial couples.
Dismissers	Ignore comments/epithets. Feel it is easier to ignore it than escalate situation. Commonly used for stares and minor remarks.
Duckers	Avoid places and groups of people hostile to interracial couples. Typically fear "safer" public places as well.
Packers	So fearful of retaliation, they carry weapons for protection.
Isolators	Limited contact with people in general. Very few associates or friends.
Prayers	One of most common coping mechanisms. Reliance on faith and God to solve problems.
Confronters	Take exception to insults, even minor ones. Typically males, but not always.
Suers	Related to Confronters. Pursue legal recourse when problems emerge. Least common mechanism in terms of use or effectiveness.

attention to it. We don't look for it and when we find it, we ignore it.

Dismiss It

Another strategy, and somewhat related to ignoring it, is to dismiss the importance of the issue. One can avoid having to respond to slights of various kinds by ignoring them or dismissing them as trivial. Consider what Adam Bruce has to say:

> We hear a lot about some of the issues—like people staring at you or making nasty remarks and stuff. But people do that to everyone, it's not a big deal. Kids do it to other kids all the time, so why should we take offense at that simply because we are an interracial couple? I mean, it's not like they are shooting at me or anything. So I don't worry about it that much. Some people make a big deal out of it, but not me.

Roy has this to say:

> We don't get too hung up on terms or issues. When others bring it up or it seems to be an issue, sometimes we sort of deal with it, but most of the time, we let it roll off our backs.

Normalize It

Still another way to deflect the pains of the insults for minor offenses is for couples to normalize their relationship. In other words, they look at their situation as similar to many other "normal" couples. Sydney Mead has this to say:

> We are just ordinary people, an ordinary married couple and go through the same things that everybody else goes through. We have our problems you know, up and down, up and down.

Greg Todd offers this comment:

> Hey look, I'm sick and tired of being singled out because I am Black and she is White. We are a married couple, that's it. Yeah, people single us out for a lot of reasons. But why can't they simply treat us like normal couples?

Awareness

At times, couples are able to minimize the likelihood of encountering problems, or diminishing their impact, by being very aware of their surroundings and the places they frequent. Many feel they can significantly reduce the type and frequency of problems by simply avoiding some places and spending more time at others. Donna Johnson comments:

> I think we are both "careful" about where we go in. There are a lot
> of places that I might go in but never with my husband, it's just
> good sense. There's no point in looking for trouble. Maybe that's not
> fair to us because we don't get to enjoy the things other people do,
> but I'm more interested in being safe and using good judgement.
> There are a lot of places around this county that we could go to and
> have serious problems as an interracial couple.

James Johnson adds:

> We try to stop at the national restaurants, you know, chains. Get
> gas at intersections. You don't know sometimes about the other
> places and it can get you in trouble real quick. Sometimes you
> wonder if you are acting this way because it seems logical to spend
> your money at a national chain, or because we don't want any
> trouble. The problem is that national chains also have problems
> with it, so there's no guarantee of that either. But I do think about
> where I'm gonna get gas. I'm not going to stop in some country place
> and get gas from a local if she is with me. I might do it as an
> individual—maybe. But definitely not when she's with me.

Hiding

A more dramatic approach is to withdraw from social interaction all
together. A number of couples say they would rather stay at home and
not be seen in public because the aggravation and fear that accompanies
their visibility simply is not worth the trouble. While being aware
implies staying away from certain places, here, whenever possible, they
stay away from most if not all public places. Donna Johnson says:

> We don't go to places that we see real rednecks; beat up pick-up
> trucks and gun racks in the back . . . really rural places.

Jimmy Schramm says:

> We try to keep a low profile and stay out of the public eye as much
> as possible. It's not fair, but it is a lot easier for us. We are both a

couple of homebodies anyway, so it really isn't that much of a sacrifice. But it is still better than risking all those problems that could come if we hung around in public a lot.

Obviously, this limits the couple's social networks, since they do not have opportunities to maintain friendships and contacts. This also places a greater reliance on families for support, however, as we have seen, some couples experience a lingering sense of opposition from their relatives.

Support Groups

Support groups are one alternative to couples that are estranged from their families, have not developed social networks, and choose to withdraw from public interaction. However, despite some evidence that some church groups attempt to facilitate relationships among interracial couples, very few are able to sustain themselves for various reasons. Consequently, many couples remain unable to develop meaningful social contacts. Russell Kenney states:

When we first moved here, I was very excited to hear about a support group for interracial couples. In the beginning certain couples were drawn to it because they thought 'I'm going to go in there and look at other people who are like me.' But as time went by you realize we're really no different from one another so it really fizzled out.

Listen to the sense of frustration in the exchange between the Sydney and Tom Mead about support groups:

Sydney: Oh the Unitarians would love it if Tom would come. But not any others [support groups] that I know of. We try to do stuff here with the Black churches, but they never really opened up to us. ·

Tom: It's important for Sydney to participate in the religion but also to have an affinity with the members of a group, particularly one that can identify with the problems we experience. We are especially sensitive to that, but we can't seem to connect with one. I'm sure if you have interracial children you need that support from both sides so I think the fact that we don't have children together might make us a little different. But there must be other people involved in these types of relationships who don't have kids . . . what do they do? I think interracial couples could benefit a great deal from some kind of support group, especially if they are parents, but there just seems to be a lack of effort made to bring these people together.

Humor

For some couples, humor is used to ease the pains of the negative reactions by others. While some instances lend themselves to humor more easily than others, a number of couples are able to find a little levity in the most distressing of situations. The use of humor as a coping mechanism also includes a self-deprecating variety, where couples amusingly poke fun at themselves or their own limitations to ease the tension. Consider Pam's observation about her husband:

> Sometimes it's good for people who are not quite sure, sometimes you can break the iceberg inward. We joke. I mean people tease us about mooning each other . . . well he doesn't moon, he eclipses, you know. Good things like that.

Karen Germaine responds:

> Sometimes you poke fun at yourself so that you deescalate the situation before it gets bad. At times, we go back and forth with each other too. Like I have this joke with him that he only married me because I'm Black and he just wanted that Black female, that slave.

> Roy: This is usually when I have volunteered to wash the dishes and as the last one is being put up.

> Karen: You just wanted that Black slave to have these kids and just do everything for you. Oh master, master . . .

> Roy: As you can see humor has gone a long way in making this work. It's important in our relationship but the studies and the reading that I have done show that in any relationship if you don't

have the humor, your chances of staying married as long as we have are slim.

Pam Williamson offers this passing dart:

I make fun because I say I married the only Black man in the world who can't dance.

Religion

A very common response to a variety of situations for the couples is the reliance on their faith as a coping mechanism. This dependence may be a function of the region of the country, where many people rely on their religious beliefs to manage all sorts of problems. However, we notice a particular reliance with interracial couples. Many couples say they rely on their faith to find their partner. Pam Williamson states:

I said a prayer and I had my list of what I wanted in a husband and I prayed for that. Somewhere, it just happened. I mean you just go down the list and it's incredible. Personality, likability, sensitivity, all of it. I mean we love to fish, to camp, my prayers were answered.

Sharon says:

I knew God had placed Brendon in my path. I had dated Black guys before, but it never really meant as much as it did when I met my husband. I know he and I are meant to be together.

Adam Bruce comments:

My wife goes to this church where there are a lot of interracial couples. I asked her what she liked most about me and she told me it was because Jesus is in her heart and in her house—meaning me.

A number of couples also use their religious beliefs as a tempering mechanism that allows them to understand the hostility and tensions that their relationship represents to others. Holly says:

I am so tired of the fighting and the bickering from other people about us. That's why in a marriage it's really not Black and White, but if you know God and you know how to discipline and love your children at the same time and do that well, they will be pretty stable. I'm not worried about someone saying something to them in school because they are going to come back here and get the confirmation they need. Even if someone makes fun of my child, if it's not about her color it would be something else.

Sydney has this to say:

People talk about my husband and I being "unequally yoked" but what it really is about, and what they are really talking about are believers and non-believers. We believe in God and there is nothing that can happen to us without his consent. We may not feel it is fair or that it is right, but we cannot question it or reject it. It happens for a reason and most of the time, it makes us stronger.

Education

While some withdraw and others look for answers in their religious beliefs, a number of couples, particularly those with college educations, attempt to use the offenses as opportunities to enlighten their fellow man to the value of open-mindedness. Many couples speak about how situations often present them with a challenge that could have implications far beyond their immediate concerns. Eric offers this comment about his need to enlighten those around him:

We refuse to respond in a negative way to people. We made a decision. If we respond and play into some of their hands, then we are not going to have any effect. We respond in a positive way. Sometimes that means it's the slow route, but it is better to educate you about multiculturalism than to beat you over the head with it. We hope you can get it on your own, but if you don't, we'll help you, but we don't push "us" on anyone.

Pam: I like to challenge a paradigm anyway. You know especially I've dealt with a lot of people who are intelligent racists. They are the hardest to break down because they really feel like they know what the deal is. I usually consider I've got several years to work on this guy and to do it in a way that doesn't offend him, even though his attitudes are offensive to me.

Pam has this to say about educating the teachers and students in her son's school:

> We did have to point out race issues in my son's school and explain that this is how some people believe and it isn't right and we don't agree with it. So when he had a problem in the school, we went to the school and talked to the teachers about the problem being "just because he's Black." The problem was really bad when we got there partly because there weren't any African Americans kids or teachers in the school. We really broke ground in that school.

Defensiveness

Still other couples become very defensive about their relationship and family situation—so much so that when problems emerge, they are quick to take offense at others' behavior. Brad says:

> Mary and I went to look for a car and she got one price and I went back and got another price. This is normal for us—we will normally go looking for things separately and feel our way around to see how they react. But this last time, for some reason, the salesman just was so obvious about it that it made me feel as though he was trying to humiliate me in front of everyone in the place. Now when this first started to happen, we would think it was kind of a game and sort of funny to see which one will be smart enough to get the best deal. But as time went on and we saw that it kept happening, we couldn't let it go anymore. We get very defensive about issues of race. Sometimes we overreact, but I think it is understandable since we get it almost everywhere we go.

> Mary: After a while you get a little tired of having to defend yourself to everyone. Some people have absolutely no tact and just start hitting you with questions that are completely inappropriate. And all the time you are wondering, 'Are they asking me this because they are curious or are they really interested or is there something else going on?' You wonder if they are honest questions or is the race card being played here. I get real defensive sometimes because

the questions seem to be implying something other than what they are asking.

Confronting

Finally, the most dramatic response, and also the least frequently employed by couples, is to confront the people who present the problem and to make them justify their actions. At times this is done to vindicate the couple by publicly embarrassing the offender or simply as a means of venting their anger at the insensitivity of others. A variation of this mechanism is to seek legal redress for some of the offenses. This is particularly noteworthy in those instances in which the partner is physically attacked by others or discriminated against by an employer. Lisa Schramm says:

> No way was I going to let my boss slide on the way he treated me. He was a racist and a sexist pig. He owned the apartment complex where we lived and asked me to be the manager. One day he sees me with my kids and my husband out by the pool. Well, all of a sudden, he's complaining about this and that, and saying that he's not happy with my work. I knew what he was doing and one day I went to his office and told him straight out. I said, 'Look, you are acting this way because I married a Black guy and have children by him. You either get over it or you can talk to my lawyer. I'll claim discrimination and harassment.' And I would have too. You can't let people like that get away with it or they'll just keep on doing it.

Russell Kenney argues:

> See, my wife does not understand what it is like to be a Black man in our society. You have to fight for every little thing you deserve. She tells me I'm going to get an ulcer. That's fine, because you know what? The only way I'm going to get my fair share is to fight for it. I've been fighting my whole life and after a while, you get really sensitive to any little thing that looks out of place. And if you don't do something about it, it grows into a lot of little things or maybe some big things, and then you have a real fight on your hands.

Greg Todd states:

I've had to get a lawyer and threaten my landlord with going to court unless he left us alone. He would show up at all hours of the day and night. He was spying on us, but he said it was to make repairs. It finally got so that I had to threaten him with a restraining order before he backed off. The guy then tried to evict us for damaging the apartment. We didn't do any damage—he was just trying to get rid of us. So we sued him and won. Then he sold the property and now we have a new landlord.

What is particularly revealing is that in some cases, the couples' reactions seem to balance each other out. If one partner reacts more demonstrably, such as a confronter or a suer, the other partner usually chooses passive methods to respond to problems. Thus, one partner serves as a tempering mechanism while the other serves to identify the seriousness and importance of the issue to the other.

Additionally, there are a number of cases in which the couple prefer to withdraw as a first option. Many couples state that they are not looking for trouble or to champion a cause, they just want to be left alone. In those situations where problems develop or they exist in some early stage of escalation, the most common response is to simply become an Isolator or a Ducker. Obviously, the easiest response would be to ignore or dismiss the slight, however, in a number of cases, the couple did not feel as though this is a viable option for them.

ASSESSMENT

One of the most interesting comments made by couples is that they are often very conscious of their visibility when they are in public. Additionally, the discussion of the ways in which some of the partners repair situations and handle problems also raises some very interesting sociological notions about people's public behavior in general.

The Presentation of Self

From a sociological point of view, much of what the couples describe is found in the work of Erving Goffman (1969). Like the feelings expressed by our couples, Goffman argues that much of our everyday behavior, but particularly our public demeanor, is based on the idea that we are all "on stage" and that we are all very conscious of our presentation of our social selves. In *The Presentation of Self in Everyday Life*, he argues that individuals are continuously aware of others' interpretations of their behavior. These interpretations have the ability to either reinforce or destroy one's positive self-image. Therefore, we are constantly performing for others in a manner we feel will be accepted as a legitimate portrayal of ourselves by our audience.

In *The Interaction Ritual*, Goffman (1967) contends that our daily interactions have been ritualized to such a degree that we have stabilized the nature of the event. Each situation, however spontaneous it may seem, has its own internalized normative order. Abiding by the rules that regulate these events provides us with a way with which to complete the interaction as well as maintaining our constructed positive self-image. The successful completion of a situation then, is based on our understanding of these norms and how well we comply with them.

A good way to understand the significance of these ritualized encounters is to use Goffman's game analogy. Each situation (or game) has its own set of clearly articulated rules. To perform well, one must thoroughly understand these rules and then acquire the skill(s) necessary to play the game. If we fail to use those skills in order to win the game, we will be embarrassed and/or encounter censure from others. Consequently, knowing and playing by the rules is a central part of sustaining a positive self-image.

The rules governing social interaction, as well as the roles we play in them, are referred to as *Lines* and *Faces*. Like any game, when a person enters, they are assigned a role. This role, or face, is the one most appropriate for the game. Each situation will define the face which is the most appropriate one to present. With this role comes a number of attributes that the person must possess if they are to successfully occupy this role. A person does this by maintaining a line—a specific action, which can be verbal or nonverbal, that supports the face the person is projecting. This is referred to as *maintaining face*.

Maintaining face is a product created out of the mutual cooperation of everyone participating in the game. There is a recognition that each player has taken a certain face and line and realizes that it is in his or her own best interest to avoid discrediting another's claim. To do so would not only discredit the person's face, but one's own as well—they are not good team players. Goffman states, "By entering a situation in which he is given a face to maintain, a person takes on the responsibility of standing guard over the flow of events as they pass before him" (1967:35). What this means is the players must constantly evaluate themselves and observe the behavior of others in order to validate their face claims.

While much of this makes sense and is a telling account about the nature of social interaction among and between people, the real value of Goffman's analysis comes from a discussion of what happens when things go astray in the interaction, what happens when the face is inappropriate or considered unacceptable to others. In *Stigma: Notes on the Management of a Spoiled Identity*, Goffman (1963) describes some of those situations in which the presentation of self is incongruous with the characteristics the person possesses. He makes a distinction between two kinds of individuals: *discredited* and *discreditable*. The discredited are those whose stigma is so obvious that making a claim of face that is different from what they appear to be is unlikely to be accepted by others. In these instances, the challenge to the individual is to minimize the impact of the obvious stigma so that the person can manage their social identity. In other cases, however, individuals may be able to present this kind of face because their stigma is not so obvious. By playing the "information game," and withholding information about oneself, the discreditable individual may successfully make a claim that may be accepted.

The two primary mechanisms used to cope with the stigmas are referred to as *passing* and *covering*. Covering applies to discredited individuals who are unable to hide their stigma. The techniques individuals employ in this situation are those which limit the negative impact of the person's face claim. Passing, on the other hand, involves concealing disparaging information about oneself in order to project a more acceptable face.

Much of what Goffman describes in his analyses can be applied to the situations interracial couples have encountered. As the couples describe, much of the public behavior involves acting and portraying themselves as normal, everyday married couples. In most cases, couples feel as though they are on display or on stage. They believe they are acting and behaving for all interracial couples and are fighting many of the stereotypical images people have of them. Reactions to their presence, either in the form of stares, hate mail, disparaging comments, or outright hostility, is evidence of their discredited standing in our society—they cannot pass themselves off as anything other than what they are. Still, the face and lines that they present are attempts to normalize their actions, as are the ways in which they handle the various problems they encounter. Resorting to tactics such as educating others or simply minimizing the significance of how people treat them can be seen as ways in which most "normal" people handle problems.

Other attempts at covering include ignoring the behavior/problem completely—as though it does not exist. Still others simply avoid places in which they feel as though they would not be welcome. Here they are not even attempting to present a face—they suspect that any attempts to minimize their stigma would be ineffective. As such, in an effort to avoid damage to their self-image, they simply avoid any type of interaction with other individuals. Unfortunately, some couples may begin to feel a sense that the number of places they must avoid are increasing. As a result, they will not only have a difficult time maintaining that self-image, but will also have fewer friends and acquaintances as a result.

For some couples, however, they are able to employ passing techniques. Some shop for automobiles separately to see what kind of reaction (and price) they will get from the sales staff. Others may simply allow people to interpret their situations in other ways without offering an explanation. Recall that a woman, upon seeing a White woman with her two African American children, thought she was the children's babysitter. During the course of the conversation, no questions were asked about the parents of the children and no information was offered. Here the woman was able to pass simply by not providing unsolicited information.

Still others may be able to physically pass themselves off as White (or some other ethnic group) which will negate some hostilities or problems. Obviously, the number of cases in which either of the latter two strategies are used is severely limited, but it does point to the various techniques some couples will use to prevent being discredited.

In sum, our understanding of the problems interracial couples experience, as well as the various ways they manage them, is clearly grounded in the sociological literature on the nature of social interaction. In the next chapter we will explore two primary sociological explanations for the continued opposition to interracial relationships and the resentment and hostility that is generated from it.

REFERENCES

Adler, F., Mueller, G. O., and T. Laufer. 1995. *Criminology*. 2nd Edition. New York: McGraw-Hill.

Gibbs, J. T. and L. N. Huang (eds.). 1990. *Children of Color.* San Francisco: Jossey-Bass.

Goffman, E. 1969. *The Presentation of Self in Everyday Life*. New York: Anchor.

——. 1967. *Interaction Ritual*. New York: Anchor.

———. 1963. *Stigma: Notes on the Management of a Spoiled Identity.* New York: Simon and Schuster.

Jaret, C. 1995. *Contemporary Racial and Ethnic Relations.* New York: Harper-Collins.

Porterfield, E. 1978. *Black and White Mixed Marriages.* Chicago: Nelson-Hall.

Seigel, L. 1992. *Criminology.* 4th Edition. New York: West.

Welborn, M. 1994. "Black-white Couples: Social and Psychological Factors that Influence the Initiation, Development, and Continuance of their Relationship." Unpublished doctoral dissertation, University of Minnesota.

Yinger, J. 1997. *Closed Doors, Opportunities Lost: The Continuing Costs of Housing Discrimination.* New York: Russell Sage Foundation.

Chapter 6

Understanding the Opposition

Many of the problems interracial couples encounter can be understood by examining the responses of family members, colleagues, and friends, as well as strangers, who contend that interracial relationships are wrong and "not normal." This is true even though these couples are *normal* in terms of their characteristics as married couples or families. What is particularly interesting is that Black/White couples appear to experience more discrimination and prejudice than other interracial couples (Billingsley 1992). In some ways, this may date back to the legacy of slavery and the overall position of African Americans in our society, but whatever the reason, Black/White couples are somehow allowed to remain in society, but are not equal participants in it.

Another important factor in explaining why interracial couples are perceived this way has to do with the negative images created by others, in large part because most people do not know much about them. Some of the hostility can be explained by the lack of contact with interracial couples, which leads to a much heavier reliance on stereotypical images of this group. Our understanding of these attitudes and perceptions of the couples by others is found in two very significant concepts: the labeling perspective and Allport's contact hypothesis.

THE LABELING PERSPECTIVE

The essence of the labeling perspective is deviance does not exist independent of the negative reaction of people who condemn it. Behaviors are never weird, bad, sick, or deviant in themselves. They are deviant only because someone or some group responds to them in this fashion. In his classic text, *The Outsiders*, Howard Becker (1963) states, "deviance is not a quality of the act a person commits but rather a consequence of the application by others of rules and sanctions to an offender. The deviant is one to whom the label has successfully been applied; deviant behavior is behavior that people so label" (p.39).

Thus, labeling theory has a different focus from the variety of theoretical explanations of deviance. Labeling theorists are not interested in the causal factors which lead an individual to commit a deviant or criminal act. Rather, labeling theory has pursued three interrelated concerns: the social historical development of deviant labels; the application of labels to certain types of people in specific times and places; and the symbolic and practical consequences of the labeling process.

The History of the Labeling Perspective

Although it was not until the 1960s that this perspective of deviance emerged as a major theoretical tradition, its intellectual origins can be traced to a 1928 essay by George Herbert Mead in "The Psychology of Punitive Justice." In it he says that the labeling process sets boundaries between conventional people and deviants. In 1938, Frank Tannenbaum used the term "tagging" to describe a similar process in his book *Crime and the Community*. He says:

> The process of making the criminal is a process of tagging, defining, identifying, segregating, describing, emphasizing, making conscious and self-conscious; it becomes a way of stimulating, suggesting, emphasizing, and evoking the very traits that are complained of. The person becomes the thing he is described as being. Nor does it seem to matter whether the valuation is made by those who would punish or by those who would reform. In either case, the emphasis is upon the conduct that is disapproved of. The parents or the policeman, the older brother or the court, the probation

officer or the juvenile institution, insofar as they rest on the thing complained of, rest upon a false ground. Their very enthusiasm defeats their aim. The harder they work to reform the evil, the greater the evil grows under their hands. The persistent suggestion, with whatever good intentions, works mischief, because it leads to bring out the bad behavior it would suppress. The way out is through a refusal to dramatize evil. The less said about it the better. (pp.19–20)

Thus, according to Tannenbaum, the stigma accompanying the deviant label may drive people into additional deviant acts.

The early ideas of Mead and Tannenbaum were elaborated by Edwin Lemert in his 1951 classic *Social Pathology*. His main questions centered around how deviance came to be initially defined. Moreover, Lemert argued that the other perspectives failed to examine the implications of being labeled. Perhaps most important, Lemert is responsible for the development of one of the most fundamental distinctions made by the labeling perspective: primary and secondary deviance. He states:

Primary deviation is assumed to arise in a wide variety of social, cultural, and psychological contexts, and at best has only marginal implication for the psychic structure of the individual; it does not lead to symbolic reorganization at the level of self-regarding attitudes and social roles. Secondary deviation is deviant behavior or social roles based upon it, which becomes a means of defense, attack or adaptation to the overt and covert problems created by the societal reaction to primary deviation. (p.17)

For Lemert, primary deviance is the type of deviant behavior that is trivial, explained away, or considered only a small part of the person's appropriate role. However, this can easily change, causing the person to adopt a deviant one. This role and the definition of oneself are affected by several factors: how much deviance the person engages in, how visible such acts are to the community, and how aware the deviant is of society's reaction. If all the answers to these questions are affirmative, then the person will see himself or herself very differently and will have difficulty holding onto his or her past self-image. As a result, the person will have to choose new roles which may be more deviant. This is what is referred to as patterned, or *secondary deviance*. Thus, while people may initially engage in inappropriate acts for any number of reasons, once caught and labeled, the reaction to deviance may itself cause further problems for the individual.

The Application of Labels

The second area of concern for labeling theorists is how labels are applied. According to the labeling perspective, the most crucial step in the development of a pattern of deviant behavior is usually the experience of being caught and publicly labeled a deviant. Whether or not this happens to a person depends more on what other people do than the individual's actions. Erikson (1964) expands on this briefly. He states:

> The community's decision to bring deviant sanctions against the individual . . . is a sharp rite of transition at once moving him out of his normal position in society and transferring him into a distinctive deviant role. The ceremonies which accomplish this change of status, ordinarily, have three related phases. They provide a formal confrontation between the deviant suspect and representatives of his community (as in the criminal trial or psychiatric case conference); they announce some judgment about the nature of his deviancy (a verdict or diagnosis for example); and they perform an act of social placement, assigning him to a special role (like that of a prisoner or patient) which redefines his position in society. (p.16)

Once a person is labeled a deviant, a self-fulfilling prophecy is initiated with others perceiving and responding to the person as a deviant. Further, once people are publicly processed as deviants, they are typically forced into a deviant group. And, as Lemert (1951) contends, once this happens the deviant will face an audience that anticipates the worst from them and this will make it difficult for the person to reintegrate him or herself into society.

Becker (1963), in examining where labels come from and how this process occurs, suggests that deviant labels arise as the result of the efforts of powerful *moral entrepreneurs*. These are persons or groups who lobby for the deviantization of certain types of behavior. They believe that behavior is either good or evil, and if it is evil it should be eliminated or "stamped out" through legislation. Once the new version of morality has been passed, moral entrepreneurs leave the enforcement of the new laws to others and usually move on to another "crusade." A classic study of moral entrepreneurs is found in Joseph Gusfield's (1966) *Symbolic Crusade*, which examined the role of the Women Christian Temperance Union and the prohibition of the sale, consumption, and manufacture of alcoholic beverages in the early 1900s.

Becker's work also examines the interaction between social control agents and individuals which determines whether or not deviant labels are applied. He begins his discussion by questioning the adequacy of the official definition of deviance. Some people engage in deviant acts, get caught, and are labeled. Still others may do it and get away with it completely. This latter group are referred to as "secret deviants."

Moreover, there are a host of factors that determine whether or not an individual is labeled beyond the nature of the act. Things such as the appearance and demeanor of the individual, the political pressures felt by law enforcement officers, as well as a host of others, must be considered.

Labeling theory also describes how deviance becomes a person's master status. While people have many statuses, the master status is the one that dominates and plays an important part in a person's social identity. In our society, one's occupation usually serves as the master status. However, once people are labeled, this changes and the stigma becomes their dominant status and they may encounter a variety of problems in dealing with other people.

Labeling Physical Characteristics as Deviant

As was mentioned in the last chapter, the writings of Erving Goffman liken social interaction to the performance of theatrical roles. Like actors on a stage, people are said to carefully manage social cues which enable them to create and sustain an impression of who they are and what they are doing. Some people however, are cast into roles which constrain their abilities to manage positive impressions of themselves. Such persons are stigmatized, the bearers of what Goffman (1969) describes as a "spoiled identity."

Goffman parallels the stigmatized problems of labeled deviants to the plight of physically or mentally handicapped persons. He extends the scope of the labeling perspective to people who are labeled for how they appear in addition to how they may act. However, this stigmatization does not eliminate a person's capacity for the aforementioned "impression management." Stigmatized persons who are creative may restrict the flow of information about themselves to those they feel they can trust.

Goffman's work raises an interesting point: we take for granted that appearances represent something deeper, they tell us about who the person is and why the person is acting in a particular way. This allows us to neatly package an individual into a stereotype reflective of their current label. Moreover, we are then able to assess the individual's past, present and future behavior in light of this new label. This is something Edwin Schur (1971) refers to as *retrospective interpretation*.

In summary, the labeling perspective has focused its attention on the societal attributes of those who react and those who are reacted against in order to explain why certain persons and not others are labeled as deviant. They argue that once a person has been labeled a deviant, and particularly if that person has passed through a *status degradation ceremony* (Garfinkel 1956) and forced to become a member of a deviant group, the person experiences a profound and often irreversible change. He or she has not only acquired an inferior status, but develops a negative self-image based upon the evaluations by others.

Consequences of Labeling

One of the more interesting questions regarding the labeling perspective is whether or not a deviant label can be removed. Theoretically, once individuals have paid their debt to society, the label is erased. However, in practice, labeled individuals are still presented with a host of obstacles which limit their ability to navigate the social landscape. While removal of the label depends to some extent on the seriousness of the offense, the long term consequences cannot be minimized. Some sociologists argue the label can never be removed, at best it can be transformed or minimized (see for instance Reiss 1989).

For instance, some people might contend the deviant can relocate and begin a life with a new identity. This argument fails to appreciate the fact that the label can reassert itself if the deviant is recognized in this new environment. At that point, the consequences and problems return. Others contend that a label can be removed based on what the individual does after being labeled. This has sometimes been referred to as *legitimating the ex-status*. The individual uses the label to help others (as in the case of a drug addict who gives lectures to elementary school children about the evils of drug use, or who becomes a rehabilitation counselor at a drug treatment facility).

Still others contend that if society changes its view on the particular behavior, then the label is removed. For instance, if a certain type of behavior is viewed as a medical problem or disease, such as alcoholism, then the person's responsibility for committing those acts is diminished. This is often referred to as the *medicalization of deviance* (Conrad and Schneider 1980). A related example occurs when society alters its moral compass and no longer looks upon the behavior as deviant. However, in each of these three examples the label is not removed: it is merely transformed. Additionally, a change in morality is highly unlikely and even in those instances in which this change has occurred, such as Prohibition, individuals who were considered criminal were still viewed that way after it was repealed.

Some sociologists contend that while removal may not be possible, recovery from the label can occur (see for instance Reiss 1989). The following factors are said to be most important in determining whether an individual can recover from the label: the seriousness of the act (with the likelihood of recovery diminishing as seriousness increases); temporal factors (how much time has passed between committing the act and the current situation); and behavioral factors (what the individual has done since committing the act). However, even this perspective has its limitations. In short, it seems unlikely that a deviant label can be removed, particularly a serious one, once it is affixed.

Thus, the labeling process has profound consequences for individuals. Our society tends to be rather unforgiving in its treatment of deviants irrespective of what they do to reintegrate themselves into society. And since we tend to be very quick to affix labels, it is easy to see how problematic this can become for certain segments of our society.

Assessment of the Labeling Perspective

While there have been several evaluations of labeling theory in the literature (see for instance Gove 1975; Smith 1975; Mankoff 1971; Gibbs 1966), most of them focus on particular aspects of the perspective. In some cases opponents of the labeling perspective have argued that it fails to provide an explanatory framework from which to understand deviance. Despite the fact labeling theory has never intended to explain the causes of deviance, many still call attention to this as a weakness. Others have focused attention on the limitations of the perspective to define exactly what theorists mean by the societal reaction. Gibbs (1966) for instance is critical of labeling theory since it does not specify what types of reactions must occur in order for the labeling theory to provide an adequate explanation.

Still others have taken issue with the perspective's inability to derive testable propositions found in most theoretical explanations of phenomena. We feel while there may be some merit to a few of these criticisms, there is little disagreement that the effects of being labeled have far reaching consequences for the individual. It is on this aspect of the perspective on which we focus our attention.

THE CONTACT HYPOTHESIS

In 1947, Gordon Allport wrote the classic *The Nature of Prejudice*. In it he describes many of the issues we have dealt with in this project: specifically how and why people mistreat minorities and other groups considered inferior. Allport begins his analysis of the nature of prejudice by describing the ways in which people in our society spend a lot of time putting people and things into categories. These *typifications*, as many phenomenologists refer to them, form the basis not only of the aforementioned labeling perspective, but they are also the basis for developing prejudicial attitudes toward people. In one sense, Allport argues this process of categorization helps us to understand ourselves and others since we have a need to explain the social and physical world. Allport also contendsour life experiences tend to form into clusters and sometimes we erroneously select the wrong clusters at the right time or the right ones at the wrong time. And still other times our entire assessment is incorrect. As he points out, this process is the primary way we navigate the social world.

Unfortunately, while sometimes helpful, this process often leads to rash decisions. Allport suggests while we like to solve problems and put people and things into categories, we also like to do it quickly. This allows us to prejudge the situation or a group of people much more easily than if we ponder the situation and its circumstances. In short, we employ cues to identify things and when enough cues emerge, we conclude, interpret, and understand, what it is and, at the same time, who we are. This makes life and the adjustments to it, quick, easy, and provides us with a great deal of continuity in our understanding of things.

Perhaps the most significant contribution this process makes towards our understanding of events and other groups in society occurs when the categories conflict with the evidence. As Allport describes, once people learn something, it is very difficult to shake them from that understanding or explanation. Thus, the categories, and conclusions on which they are based, remain fairly static. And even when those instances arise when we are forced to consider that our generalized understanding runs counter to what is actually occurring, we are very reluctant to admit the possibility of error on our part. Instead, we use the device known most commonly as *exceptions*. By using exceptions, we are able to retain our initial understanding of an event or group of people while at the same time acknowledging that differences may occur. This form of identification and explanation, along with the sweeping generalizations that come from it, are not due to a lack of willingness to understand society or the people in it, rather, it comes from an almost desperate search for all the answers. Categorizations have the added advantage that it simply takes less effort to understand things than it does to actually verify the information. And since our friends, associates, and relatives approve of our prejudgements and typifications, it is easy to see why people often neglect to learn more about a different group of people.

The linkages to this form of social psychological understanding of man in our society and its relationship to the nature of prejudice are rather obvious. One could easily argue an extreme form of the categorization process involves affixing negative or stigmatizing labels to other people and groups. However, the real value of Allport's argument can be found in the ways in which this type of labeling can be reduced—through contact with others so that these generalizations are swept aside.

Known by some experts as the *contact hypothesis*, Allport describes how contact with minorities and other stigmatized groups can actually enhance our overall understanding of them as well as improving their standing in society. However, simple contact is not enough; it must be a particular kind of contact under the correct circumstances.

While there are a number of variables to determine the effect contact will have on people's attitudes, such as its frequency, duration, and variety, there are a host of other factors we should examine. Figure 6.1 helps us identify six factors Allport considers essential in determining if the contact will likely result in a constructive or counterproductive relationship.

First, we should consider the status of the two parties involved.One factor in determining if the contact will result in a positive experience is whether or not the minority member has an inferior, equal, or superior status to others. The roles one play also have important considerations, such as whether one party is in a subordinate or superior position, as in the case of employee and employer or teacher and student. Also important is whether or not the relationship between the minority member and the other party is competitive or cooperative.

The social atmosphere in which the contact occurs is also significant, such as in the case of segregated contact, or even whether or not the

Figure 6.1
Factors Determining Relationship

STATUS	Equal/Not Equal
ROLES	Subordinate/Superior
RELATIONSHIP	Competitive/Cooperative
CONTACT	Involuntary/Voluntary
PRIORITY OF CONTACT	Trivial/Important
PERSONALITY OF INDIVIDUAL	Suspicious/Amiable Age Education

contact is voluntary or involuntary. Finally, it is important to determine whether the contact is regarded as important and intimate or as trivial and inconsequential. We should also note that the personality of the individual experiencing the contact is significant as well. For instance, the implications of the contact will be very different if the individual is fearful or suspicious of others or if he or she uses stereotypes to understand different groups. The person's initial prejudice against the group, as well as his or her age and general education level, are considered important as well. All of these factors about the dynamics of the situation are essential to understanding the nature of prejudice. Of particular importance, especially for our purposes, are the types of contact the person has with others.

Casual Contact

The first type of contact involves casual ones with other groups. This type of superficial association, which may be simply the result of a large segment of the population living in a given place, may lead others to believe they "know" what other groups are like. Allport, as well as others, have found that this type of contact not only fails to reduce prejudice but can actually increase it. In this type of interaction, the numerical size of a minority group may lead to greater contact, but this type of contact can also lead to increased conflict.

Another type of contact involves acquaintances rather than simply casual contact. A number of studies support the idea that accountancy relationships can reduce prejudice (Allport and Kramer 1946; Gray and Thompson 1953; Stouffer 1949). Much of what Allport argues is that knowledge about and acquaintances with members of minority groups result in more tolerant attitudes toward them.

Residential Contact

Another type of contact is referred to as residential contact. Here the essential point is that prejudicial attitudes and racial tensions can be improved with programs such as integrated housing. Segregation not only brings with it a host of problems for the minorities in the form of substandard housing, inadequate education, and limited social networks, but it also inhibits the overall understanding of the group by others since they will employ these stereotypical images to suggest a line of behavior that fits with their understanding of those living conditions. And, as Allport states, "Segregation markedly enhances the visibility of a group; it makes it seem larger and more menacing than it is" (1947:269).

The problems associated with lack of exposure are minimized when minorities and others live in the same neighborhoods or even in the same apartment complexes. Allport found those that had closer contact with minorities by living together found fewer differences between them and others. As he states, "The trend of evidence clearly indicates that white people who live side by side with Negroes of the same general economic class in public housing projects are on the whole more friendly, less fearful, and less stereotyped in their views than white people who live in segregated arrangements" (1947:272). However, as he correctly points out, it is not simply the fact that the two groups live side by side. Rather, the issue relates to the communication networks generated from living so close to one another. If it were so simple as to suggest that close proximity or integration solves the problem of prejudice, the solutions would be fairly easy to implement.

In short, residential contact itself is not enough to reduce tensions, but those housing policies encourage communication and friendly contact are helpful in establishing social ties between groups.

Occupational Contact

A third type of contact relates to employment. We have seen that threatened residential contact, as well as simple casual contact, does not ordinarily result in reducing tensions and hostilities between minorities and others. Occupational contacts with minorities of equal status, however, tend to reduce prejudicial attitudes among individuals. Interestingly, it also improves the relationship if the minority member is higher in occupational status.

When individuals are at different occupational levels, it is possible that the nature of this contact will be tense and even outright hostile. Battles between management and labor often find themselves racially, as well as occupationally, divided. In those cases, the nature of the contact can inflame attitudes about a particular group, especially if that contact is limited and focuses on controversial issues.

Pursuit of Common Objectives

Finally, while the effect of occupational contact (and all forms of contact for that matter) can be very favorable, people often have difficulty generalizing their experiences. In other words, they may interact with a member of a minority group, and deal with them in a manner considered appropriate while they occupy that role, but still retain strong negative sentiments toward that group. This is true even when the contact consists of parties with equal status.

For this reason, Allport suggests the only really meaningful contact is the kind in which people do things together that changes their attitudes. To underscore his point, he uses an athletic team as an example. He states: "Here the goal is all-important; the ethnic composition of the team is irrelevant. It is the cooperative striving for the goal that engenders solidarity. So too, in factories, neighborhoods, housing units, schools, common participation and common interests are more effective than the bare fact of equal status contact" (1947:276). Another good example, although Allport does not specifically refer to it, is the military. Here multiculturalism is given a back seat to the objective or mission. Successful mission completion is what is paramount, not whether the individuals assigned to that mission differ significantly. We note this trend among interracial couples in the next chapter, but the point Allport makes is a significant one: facing a common interest or objective is perhaps the most effective way of reducing prejudice and building a sense of tolerance among people.

In sum, while there are a multitude of variables in understanding prejudice, one of the most salient is the amount and type of contact that minorities have with other groups. Defined here, the contact hypothesis states that positive changes in intergroup patterns and attitudes will occur if certain conditions are met, such as the sharing of a common goal in a supportive environment, and the sharing of equal statuses among the parties involved.

As Schaefer (1993) points out, a significant amount of research has been conducted on the contact hypothesis. Most of the studies suggest that this type of contact between people of equal status in harmonious circumstances will cause them to become less prejudiced and ignore stereotypical images of others. This also improves the attitude of minority group members.

For instance, Smith (1994), in a study of biracial private neighborhoods at two points in time (1974 and 1984), found that though interracial visiting and prejudice are inversely related, more strongly for Whites than for Blacks, support for the qualifying conditions is stronger for Blacks. Ellison and Powers (1994) in a national survey of African Americans found that interracial friendship is one of the strongest predictors of African Americans' racial attitudes. As they describe it, interracial contact, especially early in a person's life, enhances the chances that African Americans will develop close friendships with Whites. Similarly, Sigleman and Welch (1993), in a nationwide telephone survey of American adults, found that in several instances interracial contact is associated with more positive racial attitudes, particularly among Whites.

Other researchers have examined the social class component of the contact hypothesis. In his study using the National Opinion Research Center's General Social Survey, Grabb (1980) found that members of the working class are less tolerant of contact with African Americans than the middle class. Additionally, manual labor workers were more reluctant than other workers to experience different types of contacts with African Americans. Grabb concludes that much of this difference appears to be due to lower education among manual workers and an overall cynical perspective of life by them than other groups.

On a somewhat different population, Caspi (1984) found that among school age children, those which had daily contact with elderly people held very positive attitudes, whereas those without such contact had ambivalent or stereotypical attitudes toward them. An additional advantage that Caspi points out is children who had frequent contact with older adults knew more about the elderly in general, as well as some of the problems they experience. As an illustration, Grabb points out that these types of children were better able to identify the age of that person with greater accuracy than those who did not have this type of contact.

With regard to equal status and commitment to a goal, a study by Braddock (1980) discovered that positive changes in people's attitudes can occur provided an equal status between the parties and the pursuit of common goals in a supportive environment existed. In this study, African American students who attended desegregated high schools were more likely to attend desegregated colleges. Conversely, those students who attended segregated high schools were much more likely to prefer colleges that were homogeneous and where other students held similar beliefs as their own.

Following the line of reasoning concerning a common goal, Hewstone et al. (1994) report two studies that evaluate programs where doctors and social workers were required to interact and work together. One study consisted of 33 medical students and 23 social work students, while the second study consisted of 41 doctors and 44 social workers. Both studies shared a learning program aimed at building cooperation in relation to a topic specifically chosen to be of interest to both groups. Both studies revealed that when these goals were the focus of the group's relationship, understanding, and increased knowledge of the attitudes and beliefs of each group occurred.

As it relates to a particular region of the country, Reed (1980) found that people who lived in the South without any experience outside this region of the country often had firm regional stereotypes. A survey of 734 North Carolinians found that southerners who had been exposed to non-southerners increased their use of conventional stereotyping, while continued exposure reduced it.

While a great deal of research suggests that Allport's insights are accurate, support for the contact hypothesis is not universal. A number of studies suggest that although research on the hypothesis in the U.S. implies that the greater the contact, the greater the understanding and acceptance of a group of people, British and Australian research contends that the opposite is true. In his study of 200 people in Australia, Ray (1983) compared the degree of contact and attitudes of working mothers, divorced people, nude sunbathers, and Blacks. In this study, there was no relationship between the degree of contact and attitude with the exception of that between divorcees and nude sunbathers. Ray's general conclusion was that contact does not have a consistent effect across all groups.

Similarly, Hamberger and Hewstone (1997) doubt the validity of the contact hypothesis because many psychologists argue that an individual who is different from the group will be rejected from the category and simply placed into a subcategory without any effect on the group stereotype. Essentially this study contends that the atypical group member is still linked to the group stereotype and is bound to affect it. Second, he contends that an atypical group member may not change the central tendency of the group stereotype but is likely to change the attitudes of some members within the group and affect the probability of applying the stereotype to an individual group member.

In examining the theoretical value of the contact hypothesis, Powers and Ellison (1995) note three primary flaws. First, most studies on the subject typically do not use populations or institutions reflective of real life situations. Many are confined to laboratories, desegregated schools, or public housing projects. The problem, Powers and Ellison argue, is that a great deal of interracial contact does not occur in these types of settings. A few recent studies have used general population samples and have differing conclusions about the viability of the contact hypothesis in the study of race relations in this country (see for instance Ellison and Powers 1994; Jackman and Crane 1986; Sigleman and Welch 1993).

Relatedly, the second criticism of the contact hypothesis is the research has focused primarily on White racial attitudes and ignored the views of African Americans. Because of the circumstances surrounding contact between African Americans and Whites, where it is sometimes competitive or even hostile, casual contact is not necessarily associated with positive racial attitudes among African Americans. Thus, there is some evidence that the contact hypothesis works differently for Blacks than for Whites and this is one area that has been neglected by researchers.

Third, one interpretation of the research on the contact hypothesis suggests that the positive association between contact and positive attitudes may be the result of a selection effect. That is, people who were initially tolerant would be the ones who would be more likely to seek out interracial contact, while less tolerant people would not. If this is true, then Powers and Ellison (1995) argue that the research on this subject has suffered from a fundamental error and there is little point in pursuing it as an area of interest. If the people who benefit from the contact would be the ones most likely to seek it out, then the contact itself has little meaning (see also Sigleman and Welch 1993).

Thus, key elements in understanding the hypothesis and in reducing racial hostility are equal status contact as well as having a common goal with a member of another group. Competition only fans the flames of tension, which can easily produce hostility. However, if the situation allows people from different groups to share a common task, the problems can be greatly reduced (see for instance Sherif and Sherif 1969). Schaefer (1993) argues, as do others (see also Ford 1986), that as African Americans and other minorities gain access to more lucrative jobs and greater standing in society, the impact of the contact hypothesis becomes increasingly more significant as an explanatory tool.

CONCLUSION

It seems fairly obvious that the problems experienced by the couples in this study can be explained using the labeling perspective as well as the contact hypothesis. The fact that so many people oppose interracial marriages and the ways people (including family members) respond to them has clear ties to the labeling perspective. For all intents and purposes, these couples are a stigmatized group. Moreover, as the labeling perspective suggests, many of the couples have internalized this stigma and have withdrawn from a significant amount of social interaction. As we have seen, one of the most common coping mechanisms to the problems they experience is to simply limit their contact with others and to withdraw to themselves.

The labeling effect is also evident in the couples' interactions with family members. Recall that one of the biggest problems the couples experienced was the lack of support by their respective families. While some did in fact support them, more commonly they ignored, ostracized, or superficially accepted the couple. Being stigmatized by society is one thing—this would probably lead them to rely more heavily on their families for emotional and social support. However, to have this group ostracize them as well only further intensifies the effects and consequences of the label.

It also seems clear that one of the main reasons family members oppose the couple's relationship is related to the lack of contact with members of the partner's race. As was evident in their comments, many couples felt the reasons their respective families did not accept them was due to a lack of understanding of their partner's culture or members used stereotypical images of them, since they did not have much contact with people from that particular race.

The contact hypothesis also seems to be a factor in understanding the problems the couples faced with the general public. While the impact or influence of the contact hypothesis is not definitive, we do believe that what drives much of the opposition to interracial couples, as well as their mistreatment in society, has to do with attitudes that are derived from both a lack of understanding of interracial couples and a lack of interaction with them. At first glance, if one examined the characteristics of interracial couples, it is clear that in many cases they mirror many, if not most, American couples—they have similar educational, religious, and social class backgrounds. The only differences of course, are the race of one partner and the way they are mistreated in society.

Thus, while our data do not consist of a random sample of the general population, and as mentioned, while we make no claim to generalizability, we feel confident that what the couples have told us is accurate and reflects a number of deep seated perceptions about them and their position in society. In fact, what we find is a group of people who, while similar in many ways to most couples, are segregated from society and their families, and are often leery of establishing friends and other forms of emotional support. This places a tremendous reliance on each other for support, which may explain, on one hand, the lack of stability in many interracial marriages, and on the other, why many of our couples have been married for quite some time.

One last factor we consider important in the discussion of interracial couples relates to the military. In the next chapter we discuss this influence as well as what the future holds for interracial couples.

REFERENCES

Allport, G. W. 1947. *The Nature of Prejudice*. Boston, MA: Beacon Press.

Allport, G. W. and B. M. Kramer. 1946. "Some Roots of Prejudice," *Journal of Psychology* 22:20.

Becker, H. 1963. *The Outsiders*. New York: The Free Press.

Billingsley, A. 1992. *Climbing Jacob's Ladder*. New York: Simon and Schuster.

Braddock, J. H. 1980. "The Perpetuation of Segregation Across Levels of Education: A Behavioral Assessment of the Contact Hypothesis," *Sociology of Education* 53(3):178–186.

Caspi, A. 1984. "Contact Hypothesis and Inter-Age Attitudes: A Field Study of Cross-Age Contact," *Social Psychology Quarterly* 47(1):74–80.

Conrad, P. and J. W. Schneider 1980. *Deviance and Medicalization: From Madness to Sickness.* St. Louis, MO: C.V. Mosby.

Ellison, C. G. and D. A. Powers. 1994. "The Contact Hypothesis and Racial Attitudes Among Black Americans," *Social Science Quarterly* 75(2):385–400.

Erikson, K. 1966. *Wayward Puritans.* New York: Macmillan.

——. 1964. "On the Sociology of Deviance," in H. Becker (ed.) *The Other Side.* Chicago: University of Chicago Press.

Ford, S. 1986. "Interracial Public Housing in a Border City: Another Look at the Contact Hypothesis," *American Journal of Sociology* 78(6):1426–1447.

Garfinkel, H. 1956. "Conditions of Successful Degradation Ceremonies," *American Journal of Sociology* 61:420–424.

Gibbs, J. 1966. "Conceptions of Deviant Behavior: The Old and the New," *Pacific Sociological Review* 9:9–14.

Goffman, E. 1969. *Stigma: Notes on the Management of a Spoiled Identity.* New York: Simon and Schuster.

Gove, W. (ed.). 1975. *The Labeling of Deviance.* New York: John Wiley and Sons.

Grabb, E. G. 1980. "Social Class, Authoritarianism, and Racial Contact: Recent Trends," *Sociology and Social Research* 64(2):208–220.

Gray, J. S. and A. H. Thompson. 1953. "The Ethnic Prejudices of White and Negro College Students," *Journal of Abnormal and Social Psychology* 48:311–313.

Gusfield, J. 1966. *Symbolic Crusade: Status, Politics and the American Temperance Movement.* Chicago, IL: University of Illinois Press.

Hamberger, J. and M. Hewstone. 1997. "Inter-ethnic Contact as a Predictor of Blatant and Subtle Prejudice: Tests of a Model in Four West European Nations," *British Journal of Social Psychology* 36(2):173–190.

Hewstone, M., J. Carpenter, A. Franklyn-Stokes, and D. Routh. 1994. "Intergroup Contact Between Professional Groups: Two Evaluation Studies," *Journal of Community and Applied Social Psychology* 4(5):347–363.

Jackman, M. R. and M. Crane. 1986. "Some of My Best Friends Are Black: Interracial Friendship and Whites' Racial Attitudes," *Public Opinion Quarterly* 50:459–486.

Kitsuse, J. 1962. "Societal Reaction to Deviance: Problems of Theory and Method," *Social Problems* 9:247–256.

Lemert, E. 1951. *Social Pathology.* New York: McGraw-Hill.

Mankoff, M. 1971. "Societal Reaction and Career Deviance: A Critical Analysis," *Sociological Quarterly* 12(2):204–217.

Mead, G. H. 1928. "The Psychology of Punitive Justice," *American Journal of Sociology* 23:577–602.

Powers, D. A. and C. G. Ellison. 1995. "Interracial Contact and Black Racial Attitudes: The Contact Hypothesis and Selectivity Bias," *Social Forces* 74(1):205–226.

Ray, J. J. 1983. "Racial Attitudes and the Contact Hypothesis," *The Journal of Social Psychology* 119:3–10.

Reed, J. S. 1980. "Getting to Know You: The Contact Hypothesis Applied to the Sectional Beliefs and Attitudes of White Southerners," *Social Forces* 59:123–135.

Reiss, A.J. 1989. Personal Communications, September-December.

Schaefer, R. T. 1993. *Racial and Ethnic Groups*. New York: HarperCollins.

Schur, E. 1971. *Labeling Deviant Behavior: Its Sociological Implications*. New York: Harper Row.

Sherif, M. and C. Sherif. 1969. *Social Psychology*. New York: Harper and Row.

Sigleman, L. and S. Welch. 1993. "The Contact Hypothesis Revisited: Black-White Interaction and Positive Racial Attitudes," *Social Forces* 71(3):781–795.

Smith, C. B. 1994. "Back and to the Future: The Intergroup Contact Hypothesis Revisited," *Sociological Inquiry* 64(4):438–455.

Smith, R. T. 1975. "Societal Reaction and Physical Disability: Contrasting Perspectives," in Walter Gove (ed.) *The Labeling of Deviance*, pp.147–156. New York: John Wiley and Sons.

Stouffer, S. A. 1949. *The American Soldier*. Princeton, NJ: Princeton University Press.

Tannenbaum, Frank. 1938. *Crime and the Community*. New York: McGraw-Hill.

Conclusion

As the preceding chapters have shown, many interracial couples face a host of problems. This is true despite the fact that, in a variety of ways, they are similar to many couples in our society. The problems they face make it extremely difficult for couples to feel as though they fit into society. Since a great deal of opposition to this type of relationship remains, particularly in the South, one might think this would place a greater reliance on the couples' immediate families for support. However, as the couples describe, this is not always possible. In many instances, family members demonstrate a great deal of reluctance to the couples' decision to date and subsequently marry. As a result, the couple must turn elsewhere for emotional and social support. This sometimes comes in the form of support groups or other interracial couples, but more often than not, the couple turns to each other. Obviously, this places an additional strain on their relationship in addition to limiting the possibility of establishing long-term relationships with others.

We have also seen that couples have a wide array of strategies to cope with the problems they encounter with others. These problems range from staring to verbal and physical attacks. The couples usually employ techniques which allow them to extricate themselves from the situation and parry the threat in an effective way. This does not mean, however, the problems go away completely or the couples feel as though they can handle themselves in these situations. Rather, in the many conversations we had with them, the couples appear to harbor a substantial amount of fear about interacting in public. Some, in fact, withdraw from social interaction as much as possible since the potential risks are simply unacceptable.

Despite these and other problems, many couples have found some level of hope in their situation and many couples have discovered positive aspects of their relationship.

ADVANTAGES TO INTERRACIAL RELATIONSHIPS

When asked about the positive aspects of being in an interracial relationship, one of the most common comments couples made was that they understood more about people in general. Roy has this to say:

I learned more about people when I married Karen than at any other time in my life. I mean, the things that people will say and do just because they don't understand really amazes me. I honestly thought that people were more understanding than they actually are. I always believed that if people were given enough information about a situation and were able to think it through, they would make the right choice. Now I see that no matter how much information they get, once people make up their minds about something, and a lot of times it is a snap decision, they will not move from that position.

Jimmy Schramm offers this assessment:

After spending time watching people's reaction to us, I think that most people are afraid of things that are different. I really do. I think we are taught what is right and what is wrong and there are no exceptions to that. And anything that falls outside of the normal category has got to be bad. Look at us, we are a loving couple who care about each other and are concerned for others and try to help people when we can. But all people see is one White person and one Black person so there's got to be something wrong or evil or sinful about what we are doing. I don't want to get too philosphical on you or anything, but I don't think people in our society are very understanding or very forgiving.

Other couples comment on a number of advantages to being in an interracial relationship. For instance, a few couples talk about activities in which they now regularly participate that they would not have otherwise if they were married or involved with someone from their own race. Consider Sean Sizemore's comment:

One of the things I have learned about White culture is race car driving! I really don't know too many Black people who sit out in the hot sun watching cars go around and around. It took some getting used to but now I kind of like it. But I know I would never, ever do this on my own.

Or consider Brad Stephenson's comment:

I had to learn how important and how involved my wife's family is to her. I mean my family is close, but Black families are huge and take on a whole different place in our lives. I mean somebody is always calling all the time and she's got a million cousins who want this, or need to talk about that. I love going to the reunions because they can have a hundred people up and they have to reserve a park or something to handle all of us. I know not every Black family is like that, but man, it is something to see.

Still another couple tries to visualize the long-term advantages of interracial relationships. Sydney Mead says:

I think the main advantage for us was the baby. I think that eventually something will be lost but a new breed will be produced in which the true American ideal will come together and focus less on social groups and more on individuals. Mixing of various kinds will produce individuals who will absorb and assimilate things from different backgrounds versus social groups. In a way, something will be lost but I think assimilation will lead to a new group of Americans who will be superior in most ways to the people we have now. I think it will continue the evolution to the American ideal.

One couple contends that there are no special advantages of participating in an interracial relationship. Rather, and somewhat ironically, they argue that where one lives has more to do with their ability to deal with the situation. Karen Germaine says:

> It's not like I grew up in a bubble or he grew up in a bubble; it wasn't like, this is the first White contact so now I see a whole new light. He does not represent every White person walking and I don't represent every Black person walking. I really don't think that there are any special advantages to being with him. I feel very lucky to have met and married him, but I don't think it is because he is White. Now some people may feel differently because they did not have a lot of contact with different races before they met their spouses. But in my situation, I have always been around White people and learned a lot about their culture, so it wasn't like I had to make this huge transition and learn a new language or anything like that.

Pam Tolbert has this to say about adjusting to life as a member of an interracial couple:

> Greenville is a good spot for an interracial couple to start out in because in Greenville you have a lot of people who have lived all over the United States. And if other people, those who do not understand different lifestyles, would just keep their focus on what they do and not pay attention to anybody else, we wouldn't have any trouble. Now I'm not saying I haven't had trouble in Greenville, because I have, but it is easier to live here in some cases because other people have seen it before. What I hope for is that more and more interracial couples come to the area and break the ice and expose people to it. That way they'll become conditioned to it and leave us alone. We aren't there yet, but hopefully someday we will.

Another advantage some couples cite are the lessons they are able to teach their children about sensitivity to others. Consider these comments by the Williamsons:

> Pam: As far as the kids go, I think there are a lot of things we can show them by being in a relationship like this one. We were talking about our skin color the other day. I was laying out in the back yard

and our daughter said 'Why are you doing this, it's hot.' I said, 'Well because I want my skin brown like yours.' And from then on she was so proud of her skin color.

Eric: That was brilliant, by the way. I told you my wife was smart.

Pam: From then on it flattered her that I wanted to look like her. It is hard to know what to teach your daughter sometimes. We try to teach them about being nice to other people even when they look very different from us, and I know how hard a lesson that is. It is hard to teach them that lesson, but hopefully our children will see that in us and imitate it when they deal with other people.

Still other couples point to the reciprocity of ideas and practices found in almost any relationship. Couples state these events or rituals enhance the ties that bind them together because they are so much a part of their partner's past or their current identity. Listen to this description by Lisa Monroe:

Of course, in any relationship I have things to offer him and he has things to offer me. He has given me insight into the Black community, things that I don't know about because I was raised White. Like this is a remedy that we used to heal a burn, on slang. And then I bring him something from my side. My mom and dad live on fifteen acres. He knows how to mow a lawn good now, he has been out in the garden and cut wood. He's from the city. He didn't do those things like petting cows. He sees that there is life outside of the city. And I see that things aren't always rosy, he's shown me things. Like pig's feet, I'll try things but that's one thing I just say no to. When we first started dating somebody had told him that people who are walking on the street were Presbyterian not pedestrians and he kept saying that and I thought he was joking. About two or three weeks ago I asked our son what you call street people and he said "homeless" so I had to set him straight too. The point is he's had to correct me on things because I haven't understood his point of view. I appreciate the fact that he can correct me and that I can correct him and we grow. Both of us are very domineering. I lived by myself for so long and it's hard for me not to be in charge. People tend to ask me to lead and he is the same way. So when we got married I made it a personal commitment for me to back down because now I have to answer to my husband. I respect his position. That doesn't mean that I don't say 'honey wait a minute I got to say what I got to say.' He will say 'okay.' That's what makes this work.

Similarly, several couples state that their partner comes from a different race, and yet is open to different lifestyles and unusual ideas, is a significant advantage in their relationship since it helps them remain sensitive to the needs of the other person and the value of their relationship. It also helps them cope with trying to understand the way racism operates in American society. Consider this comment by Russell Kenney:

> If I had to pick the perfect wife that I could have, she is very close to it. It's very hard to find a lot of fault but sometimes that's kind of frustrating because you can't live up to that and you can't return it sometimes. I consider her my equal and we've always shared things together and have both kind of compromised together even though I like to be more stubborn. We're both very approachable to talking to one another. She knows me better than anyone else and I think she helps me a lot too. I like to talk to her and trust her and the fact that we both trust each other was there from the start. I know that she is really sensitive to issues of race and that is because we have experienced so much together. But I also know how difficult that has been for her. So I always try to keep her feelings in the front of my mind. I can't do anything about my race, but I can do something about how it affects her, at least sometimes I can. She does the same for me, which means that we are always thinking of each other. That's one of the main reasons why I think we have lasted so long—we are a lot stronger because we are really sensitive to the problem. And because she is so understanding and knowledgeable, and so much stronger than I am, she has taught me how to chase away the demons that get to me about racism. I used to get so angry and be so volatile and now I realize that if I want this relationship to last, I have to let some of that go. And she has been able to help me do that.

THE MILITARY AND INTERRACIAL COUPLES

One of the most interesting conclusions from this study has been to identify the role the military plays in the lives of many interracial couples we interviewed. In fact, this was a pervasive theme in the study and we asked the couples what role they think it played in their decision to date and/or marry someone from another race. Because military service by at least one partner, or in some cases growing up in a military family, was so prominent in this study (recall that only one couple had not had any type of military experience), we also asked what role they thought it played in the lives of so many other couples.

In sharing their experiences, a few couples offered comparisons to life in Europe, and how differently Americans view interracial couples. For instance, Pam and Eddie Williams offer this anecdote about the trouble they had adjusting to the situation after living in Europe for several years:

> What happened was that we were stationed in Germany for three years. And in Germany, there were a lot of GI's and a lot of biracial marriages there. You send guys over there for a year and a half or so, and in Germany it is just so easy to adjust and get comfortable there. Especially all those single guys and within that culture there was a tremendous amount of acceptance for us and for them. And a lot of people don't stay in the part for Americans—they venture out into the German culture. And the German people are very accepting. In fact, in our case, we didn't see anyone that had any protest or problem with us in the time we were there. We came back to this country and one of the first things that happened on a road trip we got snowed into a place somewhere between Washington D.C. and Boston . . . I think it was in Pennsylvania. Anyway, it is in the mountains somewhere and the next morning there was this Waffle House and we were sitting in it waiting to get something to eat and this guy comes over. You could tell he was a Billy Bob redneck. And I mean, I knew we were going to have problems from then on. In the military and, especially in Europe, you just don't have those kind of problems.

Sean Sizemore offers this experience:

> I had a girlfriend from the time I was 10 years old until I was 14 who was half Mexican and half French in a military base setting overseas in Panama. So I was probably more isolated from what the U.S. was really like, but when I got back to the States, I guess it was sort of a rude awakening. On the base there's not really the

social separation. People all basically live in the same community.
Race is really not an issue. I didn't grow up in a Black neighborhood. My peers weren't all Black or all White so I was a little bit
more open-minded. When I came back to the States it was like you
didn't cross the lines. I think there is a sense of unity in the military
that does not exist anywhere else in the world.

Eric Williamson, himself a product of an interracial military marriage,
has this to say:

I guess growing up on bases it was not a problem but if I would go
to my grandmother's or my aunt who lived in Tennessee . . . just
the strict segregation and this was in the 1960s. Just living in a
segregated society. I can remember outside the base there were
burning crosses and I remember my dad was going to Vietnam and
this had a big impact on me and we were going to live in Tennessee
and we were driving from Myrtle Beach and my parents were really
tired and we tried to find different places to stay and couldn't so
we ended up sleeping out in a rest area. And I guess for my entire
life I grew up knowing that I was going to be treated differently in
society and that it was out there so I guess I carried that with me.

Tom Mead talks about how military life helped him deal with a wide
range of people:

Growing up in the military, in a strict military family, military
people knew how to more or less get along with each other and to
some extent with civilian people. Civilian people have more problems making changes and dealing with people different from
themselves, where military families didn't have a problem at all.
By moving to so many different places and being in so many
different schools, I had to learn how to make friends. And that has
helped me as an adult since I can talk to almost anybody. For a long
time, I felt that people were basically fair and honest and that they
treated me with the same respect that was instilled in me by my
father. Respect is very important in the military and my father
taught me at an early age to treat people with dignity. But when I
married someone from another race, suddenly people didn't want
to talk to me anymore. And in public it was fine as long as I was
alone. When I went out with my wife, I could just feel the differ-

ence—with people I knew as well as strangers. But I never felt that while living on base or near other military families.

In an attempt to learn more about the military influence among our couples and what role they thought it played in their lives, as well as in society, we asked couples how and in what way the military made them more sensitive to issues of race, so they thought nothing of marrying someone from another race. While part of it may have been that many partners spent time in Europe, either as children or adults, where attitudes about interracial couples are much more favorable, many partners who have military backgrounds offer an explanation that is similar to the one offered by Eddie Williams. He says:

My theory would be that the military is very, although racism does happen, it's neutral. Of course with my dad in the military I grew up with a very neutral attitude. But initially, I thought it [greater sensitivity] was because they don't allow it, and all the regulations that prohibit it, blah, blah, blah. It's much more than that. When I went in, and this is still true today, when I went in the military there were people from a lot of diverse backgrounds. And people don't always get along for a lot of reasons, sometimes because you just don't like them for what they are, sometimes it is because of religious reasons, or maybe it has to do with cultural differences. But we go in and get these hair cuts and they put us in the same clothes. Then they treat us all like crap. They strip away all of your personality, and everything about you, they strip down to nothing make you a part of a team, then build you up into something that they want you to be. I have seen some of the toughest people have barriers taken away to learn to fight for a common goal to save a country. And it isn't so much because you are a patriot or anything . . . it is because you'll get killed if you don't do this the right way. I mean the military focus is national, it isn't so much patriotic as it is we all have this common goal and we have to complete the mission and not get killed. So we all have a real interest in working together. Then when you come through that training you're all equal and you respect each other. You don't have to like the individual as a person, you just have to recognize that you need each other and that is more important than any personality differences.

Then you are moved all over the world to all these different places and the only people you can really relate to, especially in the beginning, are other GI's. So that teaches you to find the commonality and focus on that rather than on the individual differences. Then as you live in more and more places and deal with more and more different people, you begin to get used to change. Change isn't bad, like it is in the States. And the thing is, once you live in a lot of different places, you start seeing how common we are as a people. German people aren't that different from French people and Arabs aren't that different from Swiss people. So you begin to realize that we are people, not different nations or religions and you begin to think, 'hey, why am I worried about the fact that she is Black and I am White?' And then it hits you: the only people who are hung up about this are Americans. Nobody else really cares except us! *We* are the ones making this a problem. Everybody else is pretty cool with it. Now there are exceptions like Arabs and Jews and stuff, but for the most part, interracial relationships are accepted all over the world except the U.S., except in the military too. There are a lot of interracial couples in the military and the only time they really have a problem is when they get out and have to deal with civilians.

Thus, it seems that the exposure to different cultures in a setting that is supportive of these kinds of relationships explains how and why the military influence is common among many interracial couples. In short, the military gives them a wide breadth of exposure to different cultures and limits the chances these individuals become as ethnocentric as their civilian counterparts. In the military at least, particularly those living in foreign countries, they can derive a sense of belonging and feel as though they are a part of a larger community. Unfortunately, the same cannot be said about all interracial couples, particularly some in the South.

One of the things we thought was important was the perspective of the couple not only about their standing in society, but if they had the chance, what they would want other people to know about interracial relationships. Roy Germaine has this to say:

Well, one of the things I want people to know is that Black males or females don't actively seek out a person from a different race. It's not like Blacks are going after people making their sole dating habit a single race for the most part. We like each other as a person, so we begin dating. We love each other, so we get married. Sure I know she's White but that isn't the issue . . . I love her. That's the issue.

Sydney Mead says:

> We are no different from any other married couple. My sister has in so many words said to me that she couldn't have done what I did by marrying someone from another race, and I am thinking that I couldn't be married to her husband. He is difficult to get along with because he doesn't understand how to be a good husband or how to deal with children . . . The key to any good marriage is that I don't care what any other woman in this world does because I need to figure out what is important for me and go from there.

James Johnson concurs by saying:

> Just for people, I know that everybody has their own opinions and that is what this life is about: you have to develop your own sense of style and own sense of who you are and that is all well and good. I would not look at you and say well you just have to try and date a Black man just to see what it's like, that is not my business. I just want people to understand that if you make this conscious choice, this is who you are attracted to and who you want to be with and what your heart tells you, then you should by the same token respect my wish, my desire that this is who I love and who I want to be with. If you don't want someone to infringe upon you and your feelings then you should respect mine. It's all about respect. If somebody was hurting another person or degrading them or if it was unnatural, then I see you having your strong opinions but with something as natural as a man and a woman falling in love who want a home, a family and who want to go to church together, and have a life, there's nothing wrong with that so get over it.

Eddie Williams wants people to evaluate interracial couples on the basis of what they do rather than what they look like. As such, he asks that people do not make snap judgements about those involved in this type of relationship. He says:

> Don't judge us by the color of our skin, but by the content of our character and the way we present ourselves to you. Don't look at

me because I'm Black and she's White. Don't look at us that way. If we make total idiots of ourselves, then we deserve to be treated like idiots. But if we show you respect in every way possible then I think it should be returned. I think that is one of the biggest things. Treat me like you would want to treat your own son. I don't want you to give me anything, I just want to be treated fairly.

Pam Williamson says:

We are an example of how a group of people as the barriers are broken, not just in marriage but in a suburban neighborhood, you'll find that you're no different from anybody else. The skin color is different but you're still the same human being inside. Other people see us as interracial, we see each other not for our race, but for our personality traits. We didn't judge books by their cover, we fell in love. I want people to learn not by the cover, but by reading the book. Then we could live in harmony and peace. This nation was founded on the idea that anybody and everybody could come and live and have the freedom to do what they wanted. We have lost sight of that and placed barriers in people's way because we need to let go of the barriers that that hatred has created.

Her husband, Eric, has this to say:

If other interracial couples are considering getting married, you need to enter this thinking it through carefully. It is really hard sometimes and you will not feel connected to anybody. I would hate for someone to just jump in. When you get into a relationship like this, there is a lot more responsibility. You are held out as a traitor to your race but at the same time, the resident expert on all issues relating to your race. So you serve as an example and as a scapegoat at the same time. And everyone will come at you about the children issue . . . that if two adults want to get married fine, but think of what you are doing to the children . . . that's garbage, but you have to be ready to deal with it. And it is constant, it never goes away, so be ready for that.

Finally, Mary Stephenson offers this insight:

What I get annoyed with is the attention it gets in the media. I think the thing that bothers me the most is Sally, Oprah, Geraldo, and Jerry Springer and all these shows have people on there and they always have a problem with it [interracial relationships]. I know there are couples out there who say 'My mom hates me now,' but it seems like we keep perpetuating the problem. I wish they would have a bunch of people who have absolutely no problem with it, but they won't put that on a talk show though. Those shows bother me. I don't think interracial marriages are that big a deal in the first place, except people like to have something to complain about. And that's really true with parents of couples. There's a certain look you get when you meet the mother or father and they look at you like "What! I can't believe my son brought this person home." And then there are my friends who ask me what it's like to be with a White man. And I'm like, what's it like being in bed with anybody? But they think it's got to be different. It's not. We argue. He doesn't put the cap back on the toothpaste, he doesn't put the toilet seat down. People think it's really different and want to know how I handle it. I don't do anything different than they do, but they never get that.

THE ROLE OF SUPPORT GROUPS

Another interesting finding from this study involved support groups. Recall that we were able to identify a support group that catered to the problems of interracial couples, but the group was not very organized, rarely met, and eventually disbanded. While the problems experienced by these couples might suggest the need for some one or some group with whom they can share common issues and concerns, in addition to providing a sense of emotional support, this was not apparent with the couples we interviewed. Initially, we considered perhaps the particular support group we discovered was not well managed, which led many couples to refrain from attending the meetings. However, in our discussions, we learned that virtually all of the couples felt support groups were not needed. This was surprising since a common lament by many couples was that they felt socially isolated. In an attempt to explain this inconsistency, we realized that a constant theme running through the interviews was the statement that the couples were typical, or in their words, "normal." They were a "normal" married couple, their children were "normal" 10 year olds, they had a "normal" family life.

While this could easily be interpreted as a rationalization or defense mechanism, it may be that this normalizing process precluded any type of mechanism which focused on their particular problems. Since they were "normal," why would they need to make use of a support group for people with particular problems and characteristics? While it is only speculation on our part, it may very well be the reason these couples did not participate in support groups is it would call attention to their marginalized status in society. The very act of joining a support group for interracial couples would suggest that they are not typical or "normal." This is particularly true since most of their efforts are spent normalizing their status.

THE FUTURE OF INTERRACIAL COUPLES

As was mentioned in a previous chapter, the role of religion plays an important part in helping couples manage the problems they face in the South. A number of couples attempt to "turn the other cheek" when they are harassed or treated poorly in public by others. Some couples use their religious faith as means of taking solace from the situations they have encountered as well as their stigmatized position in society, particularly in the South. This emphasis on religion, and its importance in everyday life, is a common feature of Southern living. Thus, it is not especially surprising to witness interracial couples using religion as a coping mechanism in the South, since so many people use it for a host of reasons. However, what is surprising is how religion is used as a justification by others to oppose interracial relationships. Given the central place religious beliefs have in many Southern states, these attitudes could have a significant impact on the future of interracial relationships here.

Recently the South Carolina House of Representatives voted 99–4 to give voters the chance to repeal a ban on interracial marriages in the state. Most observers believe that the Senate will follow suit and vote to repeal the ban (Taylor 1998). What is surprising about this vote is the entire issue emerged almost by happenstance. Representative Curtis Inabinett, a Democrat from Charleston, had originally asked House researchers to review the state constitution to identify any legislation that was racially biased. Researchers discovered that the constitutional ban was placed prohibiting Blacks and Whites from marrying right after Reconstruction. However, this ban has remained unenforceable since the U.S. Supreme Court ruling in *Loving v. Virginia*. Alabama is the only other state that has retained a ban on this practice (Taylor 1998).

What is particularly interesting about this issue is not whether South Carolina should retain the law; that has already been rendered moot by the *Loving* decision. Rather, those lawmakers who are opposed to repealing the ban cite religious reasons which prohibit interracial marriages. Still others cite the repeal as another step towards a declining morality within the state. For instance, Rep. Lanny Littlejohn, a Republican from Spartanburg, South Carolina, says his views are not rooted in prejudice toward African Americans, rather, his opposition is rooted in religious conviction. He states: "It would be much better if we married our own race. Society may have accepted (interracial marriages), that doesn't make it right" (Cude and Dean 1998). Littlejohn goes on to say that interracial marriage is an example of how humanity has fallen since the Garden of Eden. He says further, "We already have the intermarriage and nobody's prosecuting. But to come out and pass a bill removing the ban is taking it one step too far" (Cude and Dean 1998). Finally, Littlejohn states "We live in the Bible Belt. If we keep on bending on things like this, we will be totally immersed in people doing what they want to do. We need some basic laws. That's not the way God meant it. He does create races of people and He did that for a reason. From the beginning he set the races apart" (Cude and Dean 1998).

In support of Representative Littlejohn, Representative Larry Koon points out: "If you go back and read throughout the Bible, there are all different nationalities of people. This is a hint that the races should be separate" (Cude and Dean 1998). Koon also states that animals of different species do not breed with each other, and as such, humans from different races should not either. He says: "You have not seen a change in the animals, the mammals, and reptiles. They have the same animals that they had when I was a little kid and that was 54 years ago" (Taylor 1998). Representative Olin Phillips states he has always believed Blacks and Whites should not marry. He states: "It's just my Christian belief that a good Southern Baptist ought not to do that. I'm a Baptist and this is a really strong, hard-shell religious belief" (Cude and Dean 1998). Further, Phillips states that he does not understand why people from different races would want to marry. What is particularly puzzling for Phillips is the attraction of White women to Black men. He states: "I don't know what prompts it. Is it the athletics in Blacks? Or is it just curiosity?" (Cude and Dean 1998).

As these and other comments suggest, there remain some deeply seated beliefs against interracial relationships, particularly marriages. These comments are clearly racist in their scope, however, the claims are neatly couched in religious terms. Each legislator cited in these newspaper articles stridently claimed this was not a race issue. In fact, opponents of the repeal assert it is not their attitude they are presenting: rather it is simply adherence to religious ideology. And who could argue with God? Many theologians also take issue with the argument that the Bible prohibits interracial marriages. Many religious scholars state that the scripture to which the Representatives point to is II Corinthians 6:14, where the scripture warns against being unequally yoked with another. However, a more accurate interpretation of that passage refers to two people from different religious beliefs, not different races (Cude and Dean 1998).

The real issue, it seems, is not that the ban should remain in place because without it South Carolinians will lose touch with their moral footing (which is hard to imagine since the ban is unenforceable anyway), or that we are violating the sanctity of religious doctrine and committing an egregious error against God (in that the scripture to which most people refer does not refer to people from different races), the real issue is racism. The fact that only one other state has refrained from repealing its ban suggests that racist attitudes remain an active part of life in South Carolina. Further evidence of this can be found in the debate over whether the confederate flag should remain atop the state capital building. However, as many sociologists point out, the racism has become more subtle, more sophisticated, or what is sometimes referred to as *symbolic racism* (see for instance Curran and Renzetti 1996). Instead of burning crosses on someone's lawn (although that still occurs at times), many southerners, even those in positions of authority, shroud themselves in the cloak of respectability when making racist remarks. Given this, it is no wonder many interracial couples feel isolated and ostracized.

The controversy surrounding this debate is an interesting commentary on our society as well as helping us to understand the future of interracial couples in the South. While racism is clearly a feature of American society, it is particularly apparent in the upstate region of South Carolina, especially for African Americans who choose to marry White partners. Thus, while we have become more sensitive in general to issues relating to race, there still appears to be a great deal left to accomplish in the South. Having said that, there is a glimmer of optimism that can be derived from this situation. As Allport (1947) pointed out, increased contact, provided it is the correct type, can reduce prejudicial attitudes toward certain groups. What we are seeing increasingly in the upstate region of South Carolina is a significant amount of growth and a rise in the number of people migrating to this area. These "transplants," as they are sometimes called, bring with them a number of attitudes quite different in their orientation than their southern counterparts. While we do not mean to suggest that Southern culture needs to be diluted on this issue, perhaps a more objective voice needs to be heard. The problems with and opposition to interracial couples stem largely from the legacy of slavery and this makes it very difficult for some Southerners to see the larger issues.

An added advantage for the future of interracial couples is something we alluded to in the initial chapters: the increased number of Blacks and Whites marrying each other. This is particularly true in South Carolina. According to one estimate, in 1995 less than one percent of U.S. marriages were between Blacks and Whites, whereas in South Carolina it was four percent (Taylor 1998). Part of this increase can be attributed to population demographics: three of ten people in South Carolina are African American whereas nationally this figure is closer to one in ten. Still, as the number of interracial couples increases, both within the state and nationally, hopefully this contact will cause the stigma to decrease in its impact.

REFERENCES

Allport, G. W. 1947. *The Nature of Prejudice*. Boston, MA: Beacon Press.

Cude, D. and S. E. Dean. 1998. "Many Support Wiping Out Mixed Race Marriage Ban," *Spartanburg Herald Journal* February 7, 1998, p.1.

Curran, D. and C. Renzetti 1996. *Social Problems*. Boston, MA: Allyn and Bacon.

Taylor, J. 1998. "House: Let Public Vote on Mixed Marriages," *Spartanburg Herald Journal* February 6, 1998, p.1.

Selected Bibliography

Adler, A. J. 1987. "Children and Biracial Identity," in A. Thomas and J. Grimes (eds.) *Children's Needs: Psychological Perspectives*. Washington, D.C.: National Association of School Psychologists.

Agar, M. 1980. *The Professional Stranger*. New York: Academic Press.

Allport, G. W. 1947. *The Nature of Prejudice*. Boston, MA: Beacon Press.

Allport, G. W. and B. M. Kramer. 1946. "Some Roots of Prejudice," *Journal of Psychology* 22:20.

Annella, M. 1967. "Interracial Marriages in Washington, D.C.," *Journal of Negro Education* 36:428–433.

Baptiste, D. A. 1984. "Marital and Family Therapy with Racially/Culturally Intermarried Stepfamilies: Issues and Guidelines," *Family Relations* 33:373–380.

Becker, H. (ed.). 1964. *The Other Side*. Chicago: University of Chicago Press.

——. 1963. *The Outsiders*. New York: The Free Press.

Besharov, D. J. and T. S. Sullivan. 1996. "America Is Experiencing an Unprecedented Increase in Black-White Intermarriage," *The New Democrat* July/August, pp.19–21.

Billingsley, A. 1992. *Climbing Jacob's Ladder*. New York: Simon and Schuster.

"Blackburn v. Blackburn," 1982. *Newsweek* May 17, p.105.

Blood, R. O. 1967. *Love Match and Arranged Marriage: A Tokyo-Detroit Comparison*. New York: The Free Press.

Braddock, J. H. 1980. "The Perpetuation of Segregation Across Levels of Education: A Behavioral Assessment of the Contact Hypothesis," *Sociology of Education* 53(3):178–186.

Brandell, J. R. 1988. "Treatment of the Biracial Child: Theoretical and Clinical Issues," *Journal of Multicultural Counseling and Development* 16:176–187.

Bruce, J. D. and H. Rodman. 1975. "Black-White Marriages in the United States: A Review of the Empirical Literature," in I. R. Stuart and L. E. Abt (eds.) *Interracial Marriage: Expectations and Realities*. New York: Grossman Publishers.

Caspi, A. 1984. "Contact Hypothesis and Inter-Age Attitudes: A Field Study of Cross-Age Contact,"*Social Psychology Quarterly* 47(1):74–80.

Collins, P. H. 1990. *Black Feminist Thought*. New York: Routledge.

Conrad, P. and J. W. Schneider. 1980. *Deviance and Medicalization: From Madness to Sickness*. St. Louis, MO: C.V. Mosby.

Du Bois, W.E.B. 1897. *The Philadelphia Negro: A Social Study*. New York: Schocken.

Ellison, C. G. and D. A. Powers. 1994. "The Contact Hypothesis and Racial Attitudes Among Black Americans," *Social Science Quarterly* 75(2):385–400.

Erikson, K. 1966. *Wayward Puritans*. New York: Macmillan.

——. 1964. "On the Sociology of Deviance," in H. Becker (ed.) *The Other Side*. Chicago: University of Chicago Press.

Feagin, J. and C. Feagin. 1993. *Race and Ethnic Relations*. Clifton-Hills, NJ: Prentice-Hall.

Ford, S. 1986. "Interracial Public Housing in a Border City: Another Look at the Contact Hypothesis,"*American Journal of Sociology* 78(6):1426–1447.

Frankenberg, R. 1993. *White Women, Race Matters: The Social Construction of Whiteness*. Minneapolis, MN: University of Minnesota Press.

Franklin, J. H. 1980. *From Slavery to Freedom: A History of Negro Americans*. New York: Alfred Knopf.

Garfinkel, H. 1956. "Conditions of Successful Degradation Ceremonies,"*American Journal of Sociology* 61:420–424.

Gibbs, J. 1966. "Conceptions of Deviant Behavior: The Old and the New," *Pacific Sociological Review* 9:9–14.

Gibbs, J. T. and L. N. Huang (eds.). 1990. *Children of Color*. San Francisco: Jossey-Bass.

Goffman, E. 1969. *Stigma: Notes on the Management of a Spoiled Identity*. New York: Simon and Schuster.

Golden, J. 1954. "Patterns of Negro-White Intermarriage," *American Sociological Review* 19:144–147.

Gordon, A. I. 1964. *Intermarriage: Interfaith, Interracial, Interethnic*. Boston, MA: Beacon Press.

Gove, W. (ed.). 1975. *The Labeling of Deviance*. New York: John Wiley and Sons.

Grabb, E. G. 1980. "Social Class, Authoritarianism, and Racial Contact: Recent Trends," *Sociology and Social Research* 64(2):208–220.

Gray, J. S. and A. H. Thompson. 1953. "The Ethnic Prejudices of White and Negro College Students," *Journal of Abnormal and Social Psychology*, 48:311–313.

Gusfield, J. 1966. *Symbolic Crusade: Status, Politics and the American Temperance Movement*. Chicago, IL: University of Illinois Press.

Hamberger, J. and M. Hewstone. 1997. "Inter-ethnic Contact as a Predictor of Blatant and Subtle Prejudice: Tests of a Model in Four West European Nations," *British Journal of Social Psychology* 36(2):173–190.

Hammersley, P. and D. Atkinson. 1984. *Principles of Ethnography*. London: Tavistock.

Healy, J. F. 1995. *Race, Ethnicity, Gender and Class*. Thousand Oaks, CA: Pine Forge.

Heer, D. M. 1966. "Negro-White Marriage in the United States," *Journal of Marriage and the Family* 28:262–273.

Herring, R. D. 1992. "Biracial Children: An Increasing Concern for Elementary and Middle School Counselors," *Elementary School Guidance and Counseling* 27:123–130.

Hewstone, M., J. Carpenter, A. Franklyn-Stokes, and D. Routh. 1994. "Intergroup Contact Between Professional Groups: Two Evaluation Studies," *Journal of Community and Applied Social Psychology* 4(5):347–363.

Jackman, M. R. and M. Crane. 1986. "Some of My Best Friends Are Black: Interracial Friendship and Whites' Racial Attitudes," *Public Opinion Quarterly* 50:459–486.

Johnson, W. R. and D. M. Warren (eds.). 1994. *Inside the Mixed Marriage*. Lanham, MD: University Press of America.

Jordan, W. D. 1968. *White Over Black: American Attitudes Toward the Negro 1550–1812*. Chapel Hill, NC: University of North Carolina Press.

Kerwin, C., J. Ponterotto, B. Jackson, and A. Harris. 1993. "Racial Identity in Biracial Children: A Qualitative Investigation," *Journal of Counseling Psychology* 40(2):221–231.

Kitsuse, J. 1962. "Societal Reaction to Deviance: Problems of Theory and Method," *Social Problems* 9:247–256.

Kivisto, Peter. 1995. *Americans All*. Belmont, CA: Wadsworth.

Kouri, K. M. and M. Lasswell. 1993. "Black-white Marriages: Social Change and Intergenerational Mobility," *Marriage and Family Review* 19(3/4):241–255.

Ladner, J. 1984. "Providing a Healthy Environment for Interracial Children," *Interracial Books for Children Bulletin* 15:7–8.

Lemert, E. 1951. *Social Pathology*. New York: McGraw-Hill.

Lynn, M. A. 1967. "Interracial Marriages in Washington, D.C.," *Journal of Negro Education* 36(4):428–433.

Mangum, C. S. 1940. *The Legal Status of the Negro.* Chapel Hill, NC: University of North Carolina Press.

Mankoff, M. 1971. "Societal Reaction and Career Deviance: A Critical Analysis," *Sociological Quarterly* 12(2):204–217.

Marger, M. N. 1994. *Race and Ethnic Relations.* 3rd Edition. Belmont, CA: Wadsworth.

Mathabane, M. and G. Mathabane. 1992. *Love in Black and White.* New York: HarperPerennial.

McDowell, S. F. 1971. "Black-White Intermarriage in the United States," *International Journal of the Family* 1:57.

McRoy, R. G. and E. Freeman. 1986. "Racial Identity Issues Among Mixed-Race Children," *Social Work in Education* 8:164–174.

Mead, G. H. 1928. "The Psychology of Punitive Justice," *American Journal of Sociology* 23:577–602.

Mehta, S. K. 1978. "The Stability of Black-White vs. Racially Homogamous Marriages in the United States 1960–1970," *Journal of Social and Behavioral Science* 24:133.

Mills, C. 1996. "Interracial Marriage Is Identical to Same-Race Marriage" in Bonnie Szumski (ed.) *Interracial America: Opposing Viewpoints,* pp.210–215. San Diego, CA: Greenhaven Press.

Monahan, T. P. 1976. "An Overview of Statistics on Interracial Marriages in the United States," *Journal of Marriage and Family* 38.

———. 1970. "Are Interracial Marriages Really Less Stable?" *Social Forces* 48.

Morgan, E. S. 1975. *American Slavery, American Freedom: The Ordeal of Colonial Virginia.* New York: Norton.

Myrdal, G. 1944. *An American Dilemma.* New York: The Free Press.

Nakao, A. 1993. "Interracial Marriages on the Rise in State, US" *The San Francisco Examiner* February 12, p.A1.

Porterfield, E. 1982. "Black-American Intermarriage in the United States," *Marriage and Family Review* 5(1):17–34.

———. 1978. *Black and White Mixed Marriages.* Chicago: Nelson-Hall.

Powers, D. A. and C. G. Ellison. 1995. "Interracial Contact and Black Racial Attitudes: The Contact Hypothesis and Selectivity Bias," *Social Forces* 74(1):205–226.

Ray, J. J. 1983. "Racial Attitudes and the Contact Hypothesis," *The Journal of Social Psychology* 119:3–10.

Reed, J. S. 1980. "Getting to Know You: The Contact Hypothesis Applied to the Sectional Beliefs and Attitudes of White Southerners," *Social Forces* 59:123–135.

Reuter, E. B. 1931. *Race Mixture: Studies in Intermarriage and Miscegenation.* New York: McGraw-Hill.

———. 1918. *The Mulatto in the United States.* Boston, MA: R. G. Badger.

Roberts, R. E. 1994. "Black-White Inter-marriage in the United States," in W. R. Johnson and D. M. Warren (eds.) *Inside the Mixed Marriage*. Lanham, MD: University Press of America.

——. 1940. "Negro-White Intermarriage: A Study of Social Control." Unpublished M.A. thesis, University of Chicago.

Rosenblatt, P. C., T. A. Karis, and R. D. Powell. 1995. *Multiracial Couples*. Thousand Oaks, CA: Sage.

Schaefer, R. T. 1993. *Racial and Ethnic Groups*. New York: HarperCollins.

Schur, E. 1971. *Labeling Deviant Behavior: Its Sociological Implications*. New York: Harper Row.

Sebring, D. L. 1985. "Considerations in Counseling Interracial Children," *Journal of Non-White Concerns in Personnel and Guidance* 13:3–9.

Sherif, M. and C. Sherif. 1969. *Social Psychology*. New York: Harper and Row.

Sickels, R. J. 1972. *Race, Marriage and the Law*. Albuquerque: University of New Mexico Press.

Sigleman, L. and S. Welch. 1993. "The Contact Hypothesis Revisited: Black-White Interaction and Positive Racial Attitudes," *Social Forces* 71(3):781–795.

Smith, C. and W. Kornblum (eds.). 1995. *In the Field*. 2nd edition. Westport, CT: Praeger.

Smith, C. B. 1994. "Back and to the Future: The Intergroup Contact Hypothesis Revisited," *Sociological Inquiry* 64(4):438–455.

Smith, F. T. 1920. "An Experiment in Modifying Attitudes Toward the Negro," *Teachers College Contributions to Education*, No.887.

Smith, R. T. 1975. "Societal Reaction and Physical Disability: Contrasting Perspectives," in Walter Gove (ed.) *The Labeling of Deviance*, pp.147–156. New York: John Wiley and Sons.

Spickard, P. R. 1989. *Mixed Blood: Intermarriage and Ethnic Identity in Twentieth-Century America*. Madison, WI: University of Wisconsin Press.

Staples, R. 1992. "Black and White: Love and Marriage," in R. Staples, *The Black Family: Essays and Studies*. Belmont, CA: Wadsworth.

Staples, R. and L. B. Johnson. 1993. *Black Families at the Crossroads: Challenges and Prospects*. San Francisco: Jossey-Bass.

Stimson, A. and J. Stimson. 1979. "Interracial Dating: Willingness to Violate a Changing Norm," *Journal of Social and Behavorial Sciences* 25:36–44.

Stouffer, S. A. 1949. *The American Soldier*. Princeton, NJ: Princeton University Press.

Stuart, I. R. and L. E. Abt. 1975. *Interracial Marriage: Expectations and Realities*. New York: Grossman Publishers.

Tannenbaum, Frank. 1938. *Crime and the Community*. New York: McGraw-Hill.

Tizard, B. and A. Phoenix. 1993. *Black, White, or Mixed Race? Race and Racism in the Lives of Young People of Mixed Parentage*. New York: Routledge.

Tucker, B. and C. Mitchell-Kernan. 1990. "New Trends in Black American Interracial Marriage: The Social Structural Context," *Journal of Marriage and the Family* 52:209–218.

United States Department of Health and Human Services, National Center for Health Statistics. 1996. *Vital Statistics of the United States.* Washington, D.C.: U.S. Government Printing Office.

Wardle, F. 1996. "Children of Mixed-Race Unions Should Be Raised Biracially," in Bonnie Szumski (ed.) *Interracial America: Opposing Viewpoints*, pp.197–203. San Diego, CA: Greenhaven Press.

Williamson, J. 1980. *New People: Miscegenation and Mulattoes in the United States.* New York: The Free Press.

Wirth, L. and H. Goldhamer. 1944. "The Hybrid and the Problem of Miscegenation," in O. Klineberg, *Characteristics of the American Negro.* New York: Harper.

Woodson, C. G. 1918. "The Beginnings of Miscegenation of Whites and Blacks," *JNH* 3: 335–353.

Wright, L. 1994. "One Drop of Blood," *The New Yorker* July 24, p.1.

Index

About the Authors

ROBERT P. McNAMARA is Assistant Professor of Sociology at Furman University, in Greenville, South Carolina. He has published numerous scholarly articles and several books, including *The Times Square Hustler: Male Prostitution in New York City* (Praeger, 1994), *Social Gerontology: Selected Readings* (edited with David E. Redburn, Auburn House, 1998), and *Police and Policing: Second Edition* (edited with Dennis J. Kenney, Praeger, 1999).

MARIA TEMPENIS is currently pursuing her doctorate in Sociology at Vanderbilt University. She has published articles on race, religion and policing, homelessness, and urban redevelopment.

BETH WALTON is currently in the Master of Social Work program at the University of Georgia. After obtaining her M.S.W. she plans to practice as a medical social worker.

ISBN 0-313-30962-0

90000>

EAN

9 780313 309625

HARDCOVER BAR CODE